Hercules Massi

Sculptures and Galleries in the Vatican Palace

Second Edition

Hercules Massi

Sculptures and Galleries in the Vatican Palace
Second Edition

ISBN/EAN: 9783337243197

Printed in Europe, USA, Canada, Australia, Japan

Cover: Foto ©Thomas Meinert / pixelio.de

More available books at **www.hansebooks.com**

SCULPTURES AND GALLERIES

IN THE

VATICAN PALACE

BY

HERCULES MASSI

THE SECOND EDITION CORRECTED
WITH CONSIDERABLE ADDITIONS AND IMPROVEMENTS

ROME
PRINTED BY SINIMBERGHI
1872

PREFACE

———— —— ———

The Vatican Museum enjoys such celebrity throughout the world, as to attract the attention of the
learned, and to excite the admiration of all stran-
gers, visiting this Metropolis. Indeed the richness,
and magnificence of this immense building, far
surpass even its fame, which not only equals,
but even excels that of the most splendid, and
most sumptuous Museums of both ancient and
modern palaces. It owes its origin to the great
Pontiffs Julius II. Clemens XIII. and XIV; but
Popes Pius VI. and VII the promoters and resto-
rers of the fine arts, have by their munificence,
contributed more than others to its present grandeur Pius VII. materially increased it by the addition of a new wing, known under the name of
« Braccio Nuovo » which is set apart for the
more remarkable statues, and also by the construction of new Halls and Galleries, decorated
with the richest and choicest monuments of art,
most excellently disposed and arranged.

Masterpieces and tresaures of Greek Art,
have been here placed side by side with the rich

and superb monuments that formerly adorned the
Forums, Circuses, Baths, Theatres, Nymphæa,
Sepulchres, Amphitheatres, and other splendid
edifices of ancient Rome. As a whole and in de-
tail, this collection is of the highest interest both
to the learned archæologist and to the lover and
connoisseur of art, who amid such a variety of
objects, will find abundant mater to satisfy their
intelligence, study, and admiration.

To the predilection of Pope Gregory XVI for
Etruscan and Egyptian antiquities, we are indebted for the formation of interesting collections of
these particular departments.

His glorious Successor, the reigning Pope
Pius IX, has distinguished himself by the restoration and renovation of the formerly decaying
Arazzi or Tapestries, by the addition of new
objects, and monuments of art, and also by the
embellishment and decoration of many Halls and
Galleries.

It would be too long and tedious to give a
minute description, and particular account of every
single object collected in this Museum. The best
work known on it, is that compiled by the celebrated antiquarian *Emnto Quirino Visconti*, who
was both the first director, and chief arranger of
this Museum. This work however, by reason of
its cost and size, is not within the reach of every
one. This induced me to publish the present volume, which aimed at a plain and brief description
of the principal and most note worthy objects.
But in printing this new edition it is my design
nothing to omit, but to render it complete with

regard to the monuments of sculpture, by adding what in the first was wanting. What does but little interest the visitor, I shall only point out, stating the place where it may be found, and discovered. To this I add a more accurate description of the Etruscan and Egyptian Museums, of the Arazzi, and Geographical Maps.

Many corrections and ameliorations will be found, so that it will I trust, give pleasure and satisfaction to the learned traveller.

The whole is divided into seven parts disposed in the following order:

1st. The New Arm - or *Braccio Nuovo* -

2nd. The Chiaramonti Museum.

3rd. The Pio-Clementino Museum, which embraces the *Portico di Belvedere*, the Hall of the Animals, the Gallery of Statues, the Hall of Busts, and the Cabinet of Masks.

4th. The Hall of Muses, the Round Hall, and the adjoining one known by the name of the Greek Cross, that of the Biga, and the Gallery of Vases and Candelabra.

5th. The *Arazzi*, and Geographical Maps.

6th. and lastly. The Etruscan and Egyptian Museums.

The additions which enrich this immense theatre of arts, especially those from the recent excavations of Ostia and other celebrated discoveries, will I hope, give to this newly improved explanation of mine, a greater interest than those which preceded it, have obtained.

HERCULES MASSI.

On reaching the first story of the lower *Loggia* constructed by the architects *Guglielmo da Majano* and *Bramante Lazzari*, with decorations of *Giovanni da Udine*, a pupil of Raphael, under popes Paul II Julius II Leo X and recently renovated through the munificence of Pope Pius IX by *Prof.ʳ Mantovani*, we enter the Museum by the iron grating adorned with crystals, which stands at its opposite extremity, leading to the:

CORRIDOR OF INSCRIPTIONS

A large passage * containing a rich and select collection of both pagan and christian inscriptions, excellently classified by the learned *Monsig.ʳ Marini*, by order of Pius VI. This double series of inscriptions particularly deserves the attention, and study of the philologist. On the right hand are placed all the pagan inscriptions relating to the title indicated above on each section. They consist principally in epitaphs of fathers and sons, brothers and sisters, pupils, husbands and wives etc. Some designate various professions and trades, such as the · *jumentarius* · a horse driver, the physician, the *nummularius* or banker, the

---

* 381 Yards in lenght.

8

wine merchant *negotiator vinarius, naricularius corporis maris Hadrialici,* the boatman of the Adriatic Sea Company; *invitator,* an agent, *marmorarius,* a stone-mason ; *lanio* the butcher etc. Those deserving more notable interest, relate to the Consuls, Magistrates, Officers of the imperial household of Augustus as that of « *Cæsaris Præsignator* » the imperial notary; also to the Minister of the Gods and Goddesses, a distinction of prizes to various military chiefs, tribunes, and cavaliers, as the bestowing of the public horse, the civic and mural crowns etc. Others deserve particular attention for the beauty of their style and tenderness of expressions [1], as well as for their semibarbarous latinity, showing the decay of the language. One of the principal is that which stands at the end of the corridor, and alludes to the beautiful restoration of the « *Clivus Martis* » made at the public expense. The section opposite the Library is full of various monuments found at Ostia, amongst which are basreliefs and epigraphs, relating to the worship of the God Mithras.

The greater part of the latin and greek inscriptions arranged on the left side were removed here from the catacombs and other ancient cemeteries of Rome. They present a striking contrast to the opposite pagan inscriptions. Instead of vain prayers to the gods, invocations to the earth to lie softly on the relics of the dead, uttered by a thirsting spirit, we find touching expressions of

[1] as : *Maccus* an innocent child, the tale of misfortune of the unhappy *Anthos*, crushed by chariots, dragged by infuriated oxen. The handsome *Maximus* torn from his mother's bosom etc.

a pure faith; allusions to rest in perpetual peace, a happy state beyond the grave, an everlasting love in the eternal life.

Symbolic signs and representations add great power to these expressions as the usual monogram ☧ in the peace of Christ, the wine, the fish, the dove with an olive-branch, Noah's ark, the anchor of hope, the Good Shepherd bearing the lost sheep, birds pecking at the mystic grapes, mysterious chalices and flasks of the blood of Christ, and of the Martyrs.

Although the style of these inscriptions is that of a decayed language, yet the formulas and sepulchral rites, the chronology of the consular « fasti » , and of the early centuries of the Christian era, render these inscriptions both interesting and note-worthy.

Lower along the walls, before the windows are arranged some important architectural fragments, amongst which there is a magnificent one in a long frame, higly deserving the study and attention of young architects, and also statues, cippi, torsi, and aediculae from Ostia.

Among the other objects of this long corridor, those considered as worthy of a particular attention are the following ones :

* An aedicula sacred to Venus Aphrodite found at *Todi.*

** A large mouth of a well « *puteale sigillatum* » exhibiting a representation of the *Mela Sudans*

* Comp. XI.
** Comp. XIII. right side.

with lions devouring horses, in high relief —
Sarcophagus with representations of boar. hunting — * Another very remarkable one found on
the Appian way in 1817. On the cover lies a
sleeping child, with a crown in his left hand.
The inscription relates to the lamented child *Marcianus*, who died under *Lucius C. Severus and
T. Auy. Fulcius Consules* in the year of Rome 873 — A ** large cippus bearing the name of
Lucius Cornelius Alimetus, a iron founder. The
basreliefs wich adorn both the sides, represent
his manufactory and customers. It is very interesting and was discovered in the *Via Nomentana*
near *Sta. Agnese*. — A niche of marble with emblems relating to Neptune, from *Todi*. On this is
another frontal of a niche bearing an inscription
dedicated to the Genius of a Centurian, made during the consulship of *Commodus aad Burrus*
in the year 181. of the present era — A figure
of a *laris*, a householdgod having the bulla hung
on it by a child, after its having put on the prætesta. Some fine architectural basreliefs of the
time of Augustus, sarcophagi, marble vases etc.

In fine, this collection for vastness and richness, does honour to the illustrious Pontiff Pius VII
because, *** bare and unadorned as this corridor
formerly was, it has been now by his munificence
fitted up with such extraordinary care, as to be
a worthy receptacle for so many valuable monuments of ancient times.

* Comp. VI.
** Comp. XVI.
*** It contains more than 3000 specimens. The Christian inscriptions amount to upwards of 1100.

THE "*NUOVO BRACCIO*"

A little beyond the entrance of the *Chiaramonti* Corridor we enter this "*Nuovo Braccio*"
of the Museum. Its exterior frontispiece is decorated on each side with two columns of bigio granite supporting busts of Augustus and Trajan
with heads of black basalt, cuirass, and drapery
of flowered alabaster, and african *bigio*. The interior, on passing the rich iron-grating, is adorned
with jambs of Sicilian jasper with composite capitals, like those of the tower of Andronicus at
Athens. This magnificent department of the Museum was erected by Pius VII from the designs
of the skilful architect Raphael Stern , and ornamented with the statues then purchased and recovered from the French Government by that
Pontiff. It was begun in 1817, and opened for
the first time to the public in 1822. It measures 313. palms in length by 56 in breadth. It is
very well lighted by twelve large skylights pier-
ced in the vaulted ceiling which is decorated with
stuccoes and *rosoni*. The *cupola*, *tholus*, in the
centre, is majestically supported by eight fine cc-
lumns of carystian or *cipollino marble*, remarkable
for the beauty of its veins, and admirable dispo-
sition of the strata. Similar columns also line the
entrance, and the opposite extremity of this wing.
Modern basreliefs in stucco, beautifully moulded

and copied, by *Sig.*[r] *Laboureur* from the columns
of Antonine and Trajan are arranged along the
lateral walls above the niches. They represent
bacchanalian feasts, triumphs, and sacrifices.

The statues are placed in corresponding niches, and a noble series of more than 30 busts,
each standing on half pillars of sienite or egyptian red granite, encircle the gallery. The floor
is inlaid with ancient marbles, and various black
and white mosaics.

  * N. B. *The numbers marked with the aste-
risk indicate the objects placed above on brackets,
or set in the lateral walls.*

  Beginning on the right:

  * *Above the entrance: Achilles dragging the
dead body of Hector under the walls of Troy. A
basrelief.*

1. Dyonisian Hermes, in penthelic marble.
2. 4. Unknown bust and head.
3. Female head, in *palombino* marble.
5. CARYATID — A statue supposed to be one
of those which supported the portico of the Pan-
droseium at Athens. When Stewart made his visit
to Greece, one of the six celebrated statues of
Cariatides, which served for the architectural
ornament of that temple, was already wanting.
By some also this statue was believed to be one
of the Cariatides of *Diogenes* of Athens. The
workmanship is of high greek style, and it perhaps may be one of the six renowned originals
of Phydias, as the majestic style of that eminent
artist is perceptible in it. It was brought to Venice by the doge *Morosini* in the XVII. century

together with the fragment of the frieze of the Parthenon, which now stands in the *Chiaramonti* Corridor. The statue was purchased by *Camuccini*, and the head and forearms were restored by *Thorwaldsen.*

  * *Above the second niche is a basrelief representing women with sacrificial instruments.*

6-7. BUST unknown — Head of Melpomenes, the Muse of Tragedy.

  * *Bacchus and Ariadne with dancing Fauns and Bacchantes.*

8. COMMODUS. A statue larger than life in penthelic marble. It is very interesting, as statues of this emperor are very rarely met with, the majority having been destroyed after his death, by order of the Senate. This unworthy successor of Marcus Aurelius is here represented as dressed in his favourite costume as a hunter with a short tunic, holding a lance in his left hand.

9. CAPTIVE DACIAN KING. Colossal head, one of the many that adorned the forum of Trajan. It is very remarkable for its fierceness and rudeness of expression. It stands on a half pillar of red oriental granite.

40. PALLAS. A bust.

11. SILENUS with the infant Bacchus in his arms. The fosterfather of the son of Jupiter and Semele, is here gracefully smiling as he contemplates his infant charge, while resting against the trunk of a tree adorned with grapes and vine leaves. The slender proportions and the delicacy of the limbs of this Silenus, the gracefulness of his posture, the swelling of the veins of the

hands and arms which sustain the handsome
infant, form altogether a most pleasant and admirably executed group.

       • *Triumph of Septimius Severus, in which the
emperor in seen crowned by a winged Victory.
A basrelief.*

12-13. Male and female busts unknown.

14. AUGUSTUS. The protector of the arts and
literature is here represented in a statue larger
than life of parian marble. The majesty of this figure fully represents the Lord of the world. On the
artistically sculptured cuirass are engraved in
basrelief, some figures relating to the achieve-
ments of this emperor : the Heaven under the
personification of a bearded old man; *Aurora* and
Hesperus preceding the Sun who stands in his
chariot, symbolising Augustus raised up as a new
sun to illuminate the Earth. In the middle stands
a warrior, perhaps a Parthian King, in the act
of saluting the Sun before consigning the Imperial
Eagle to Tiberius, or to the General, who stands
before him with a dog, the symbol of fidelity. On
the right and left side of this central group, are
seated two figures representing Hispania and Gal-
lia, provinces subdued by Augustus. Below them
are Apollo seated on a griffin, and Diana on a
stag, to represent the victory of Actium, where a
temple was dedicated to this god, and the recovery
of Sicily sacred to Diana. Below, the Earth is
seen personified with its children, an allusion to
the peace rendered by this emperor. Lastly the
two sphinxes sculptured on the shoulders indicate
the conquest of Egypt, and the Cupid on a dolphin,

the origin of the emperor from Venus, or better
his naval conquests.

This highly esteemed statue was found in the
beginning of the year 1863. eight miles beyond
the Porta del Popolo at *Prima Porta*, the first
Roman station " *ad Saxa Rubra*" on the Flaminian way, in the ruins of the villa of the empress
Livia, called *"ad Gallinas"*. It is perhaps the work
of some greek sculptor attracted to Rome by the
munificence of that Prince. It has been carefully
restored by *Com.ᵣ Tenerani.*

*On the floor before this statue is inlaid an
ancient white and black mosaic representing Ulysses, who lashed to the mast of his galley escapes
from the deceitful and bewitching songs of the
Syren Parthenope, a monster half-woman half-fish,
which is playing on the lyre. On the opposite side of
Carybdis, stands Scylla beating with the oar two
wrecked men, who are devoured by her dogs. On
the other side the nymph Leucothoe is seated on a
sea monster, while Palemon, a little child, is
spurring on a monstrous fish. The design and
composition is good. It was found in the excavations of Tor Marancio.*

15. UNKNOWN male bust with cuirass, supposed to be Didius Julianus. It came from the Ruspoli
Gallery.

16. Colossal beardless bust.

17. ÆSCULAPIUS. A fine beardless statue of
the God of Physic. With more probability, it is
thought to represent Antonius Musa the phisician
of Augustus, the first who prescribed the use of
the cold bath, by which he restored the health

of this Emperor, who in gratitude erected a bronze
statue to him. The serpent twined round the trunk
by which this statue is supported, is an emblem
of wisdom, necessary to the followers of the healing art.

    *Dancing Fauns and Mænades carrying the
infant Bacchus in his cradle. A basrelief.*

18. CLAUDIUS, bust found at Piperno.

19. Bust of Amazon.

20. NERVA. This well preserved statue dressed
with the consular toga exhibits to us the image
of that good emperor, whose virtues did honour
to the throne.

    *Drunken Silenus supported by Fauns. A bas-
relief.*

21-22. FEMALE and male busts with chlamys.

23. PUDICITIA. A closely veiled statue of the
goddess of Modesty, or, perhaps, a portrait-statue
of some Roman empress or Matron. The right
hand is lightly wrapped in the rich and well preserved folds of the graceful drapery, the left,
appearing through the delicate veil, supports the
head, which, though of modern workmanship
highly expresses a beautiful majestic, and dignified
countenance. This very remarkable monument of
greek art, was brought here from the Villa Mattei
on the Cælian Hill. Pliny speaks of a *signum* or
statue, erected to this divinity in the Roman Forum, and its image has been frequently represented on ancient roman coins, with the same attributes of Modesty.

    *Passing the column above: Priestesses ador-
ning a candelabrum with festoons and garlands
of flowers. A basrelief.*

24-25. Castor and Pollux sons of Leda and Jupiter. The nebrys on the shoulder of the first one is in rose alabaster.

26. *In the niche :* TITUS. In looking at this statue we see in it the image of an emperor, who by the wisdom and beneficence of his government was the delight of mankind. The figure agrees well with the general appearance of the individual represented. The drapery is finely arranged. The honey-comb at his feet is a fine allegory of the sweetness and goodness of the character of this prince. It was discovered near the Lateran in 1828.

27. *At the four corners of the Hall are co-lossal masks of Medusa in a good style supported by porphyry columns. See Nᵣ 40. 93. 110. Nᵣ 22 and 40. were found in the discovery of the temple of Venus.*

28. SILENUS, a statue.

29. Faun carrying a child. A statue.

*Passing this statue on the right side we come to a tribune, to which we ascend by steps. It opens on the garden della Pigna by a bronze-grating decorated with two columns of white oriental ala baster, and two of giallo antico, discovered at Ac-*qua Traversa *on the Cassian way, where Lucius* Verus *had a villa.*

In the niches down the tribune:

30. A smiling Faun. A good sculpture.

31. PRIESTESS OF ISIS represented with *ca-lamistrati* or curled hair, crowned with the lotus-flower, holding in her hands the *aspergillum*, and a vase for the *aqua lustralis*, or water of pu-rification. It is the work of a greek chisel, but

executed perhaps at Rome about the time of Hadrian.

32-33. *At each extremity of the base of corallina breccia of the parapet, there are two statues
numbered 32 and 33 representing:*

FAUNS seated on leather wine bags, looking
at the bunches of grapes held in their hands: Found
in the villa of Quintilius Varrus at Tivoli.

34-35-36. *On the parapet of a fine broccatello of
Spain, stand skilfully arranged handsome figures
of a FAUN, THETIS, and VENUS ornamented
with necklaces, and seated on hippocampi.*

Down in front of the parapet:

37. STATUE of a poet crowned with laurel, in
pontelic marble.

38. GANYMEDE. The handsome cup-bearer of
Jupiter, stands in a graceful posture, as pouring
into the cup the libation for the Gods. This statue
is undoubtedly an exquisite piece of greek workmanship as may be seen by its epithet of illustrious - PHAIDIMOS, engraved on the trunk of
the tree which supports the figure. It probably
served to adorn some fountain, and was found in
a *Calidarium*, or bathing room at Ostia, in the
beginning of this century.

In the middle of the Hall stands:

39. A SUPERB COLOSSAL VASE in a very
elegant etruscan style wrought in black egyptian
basalt. Instead of handles two ferula stems encircle the vase adorned with thyrsi, pine-leaves
and cones, a wreath of Acanthus, and bunches of
grapes at which birds are pecking. It was disco-

vered in fragments near St. Andrea on the Quirinal Hill, and afterwards admirably restored.

The Mosaic on which this large vase stands, represents Dionysiac masks, with dancing Fauns at the angles. It was found as the others at Tor Marancio.

40. See *N^r 27.*

41. *In the niche* : FAUN. A small figure resting against the trunk of a tree partly covered with a tiger's skin, playing on its rustic instrument. It its remarkable for its good style. It was found near the lake of Circeii in the villa of Lucullus, as the inscription engraved on its base shows.

Passing the column, above:

* *Bacchus supported by Fauns and Bacchantes. A basrelief.*

42. Bust unknown of a Roman Lady. The hairdress points the time of the Flavians.

43. Julia Soemia, bust.

44. WOUNDED AMAZON. An interesting statue of one of those warlike women of Thrace perhaps their queen Hippolita. The artlessly parted hair, and the beautiful attitude in which she stands raising the arm and showing a wound in her right breast, is admirably expressive of physical pain, and of the grief she feels at having been vanquished. On her back she carries the bow and the quiver. This fine statue is perhaps a copy from the celebrated original of *Ctesilas*, a greek sculptor.

45. Bust unknown with drapery in oriental alabaster.

46. Bust of Plautilla, the wife of Caracalla.

47. CARYATID. A statue remarkable for its monumental character and exquisite workmanship. It formerly stood in the villa *Negroni* on the Viminal, and it is a work by *Criton*, a copy from the celebrated original of Phydias.

48. Trajan with the chlamys and baltheum a remarkable bust.

49.* Head of Maximus, successor of Alexander Severus.

50. DIANA. A statue. The chaste goddess of the chase is represented in the act of amourously looking at the sleeping Endymion whose figure is wanting. It is supposed to have been formerly connected with the present statue as forming part of the group. The tender and graceful expression of love and admiration shown in her countenance, the slender proportions of the body, the gentle bending, and the noble posture of the figure, form the value of this fine composition. It was found in a farm beyond the *Porta Cavalleggeri.*

   * *Triumph of M. Aurelius with the representation of the passage of the Danube, and the image of Jupiter Pluvius , to indicate the miracle of the rain, obtained on that occasion by the Theban legion, to quench the thirst of the troops.*

51. Bust supposed to represent Macrinus.

52. Bust of a Roman Lady of the time of Adrian.

53. EURIPIDES. A statue. The great luminary of the tragic poets is represented as holding a scroll of papyrus in his left hand, while the right supports the well arranged *pallium* and the tragic

mask. On the spacious forehead there is a marked
expression of intellectual power, whilst the veins
and the muscles of the hands, the breast and arms
in their tragic simplicity exhibit something of an
herculean character. It was formerly in the Giustiniani palace.

*Inlaid in the pavement: PROTEUS surro-
unded by various seamonsters. A fine white and
black mosaic.*

54. MARCUS MAXIMUS PUPIENUS. An excellent portrait bust.

55. Manlia Scantilla, the wife of Didius Julianus.

56. JULIA the daughter of TITUS, expressed
under the attributes of Clemency. A statue of
good roman workmanship. It came from *Camuccini's* collection.

57. LUCIUS CORNELIUS CINNA ? A bust.

* *Mœnades assisting at a nuptial feast. A b. r.*

58. Julia Soemia, a bust.

59. Statue of Plenty, in greek marble.

60. Bust supposed to represent Silla, the famous
dictator.

61. Faustina, the wife of Marcus Aurelius, a
bust.

62. DEMOSTHENES. A statue full of admirable energy, and one of the finest of this collection. The greek artist appears here to have se-
lected the moment in which the great orator is
indignantly declaming against the fickleness of
the Athenians, who refuse to listen to him, while
he advocates the rights of their country, against
Philip their oppressor. As both hands and forearms have been restored, this opinion does not

agree well with the present attitude of the statue; but originally they were opened and raised up, as expressive of animated gestures in the warmth of speech.

The disdainful countenance, the act of unfolding the scroll, the pallium artistically encircling the seminude figure, the peculiar elevation of one lip, and the compression, them of both highly express the vigour and strength of his manly eloquence. It was discovered at *Frascati* in the *Aldobrandini villa*.

* *Above the iron grating which communicates with the north corridor of the adjoining Library: Ulysses drawing the bow, and taking his revenge against Penelope's suitors.*

Before the same grating in the middle:

63. Ælius Cæsar? Bust from the Ruspoli Gallery.

64.* 66. Busts of unknown roman Ladies.

65. Mercury, a hermes with emblems wanting.

67. APOXYOMENOS, or ATHLETE. A semiheroic statue standing as in the act of cleaning his right arm from the perspiration and dust with the strigil, a metal instrument used in the circuses for this purpose. In the other hand he holds a dice, an unwarranted and improper modern addition. The sculpture is a masterpiece in every respect, and the figure is full of life. It is perhaps one of the finest repetitions of the celebrated bronze original statue by Lysippus, which Pliny tells us, having been removed by Tiberius from the baths of Agrippa to his own palace, was after a sedition of the people in the theatre,

restored to its former site. It was found in the *Vicolo delle Palme in Trastevere* in 1849.

A 67. Hercules, a hermes found at Ostia.

68. Marcus Aurelius in his youth, a bust.

69. Remarkable bust of an Orator.

70. Bust of the young Caracalla.

* *Sacrifice to Diana with women imploring her aid. A basrelief.*

71 AMAZON. A very remarkable statue. Some suppose it may also represent *Camilla* the Volscian queen wounded in the breast by the Etruscan Tarchon, *Tarquinius.* This supposition is greatly strengthened by the different style and execution, and the spur, wich Amazons bear, on the left foot.

72. Draped bust of PTOLEMY son of Juba king of Numidia, and Mauritania, who when a mere boy was led to Rome, to adorn as a captive the triumph of Cæsar after the victory of Pharsalia. It stands on a pillar of red oriental granite.

* *Women dancing to the sound of musical instruments. A basrelief.*

* *Triumph of Titus in which the spoils of the temple of Jerusalem, are seen carried in tr iumph. A basrelief.*

73. Roman Lady, perhaps Matidies the niece of Trajan.

74. Clemency, a statue in a good style.

75. Bust of a roman personage of the time of the Antonines.

76. ALEXANDER SEVERUS. A bust.

77. ANTONIA. A statue found amongst the ruins of Tusculum, easily known by the physiognomy and the arrangement of the hair to be the wife

of Drusus the Elder, and the mother of Germanicus. The folds of the drapery are agreeably distributed. According to the custom of the ancient Romans and Greeks she bears a ring on the little
finger of her left hand. The marble is the *grechetto*.

78-79-80. Roman Ladies. Bust N.ᵒʳ 79. perhaps
is allusive to Venus Eustephanos, or Sabina, the
wife of Adrian.

81. Adrian, a bust adorned with the.

82. Pallas, bust with the ægis.

83. CERES. A valuable semicolossal statue found
in fragments. The upper portion has been skilfully
restored by *Cav.ʳ Pietro Galli*. The emblems of
the ears of corn and poppies in her hand as well
as the swelling bosom, undoubtedly prove it to be
a Ceres *Mammosa*. It was found at Ostia near the
Thermae Maritimae Sea-Baths, one of the richest
and most sumptuous edifices of that ancient and
renowned city.

84-85. Busts unknown.

86. FORTUNE. The celestial dispenser of riches
is represented in a statue larger than life. The
rudder in her right hand and the cornucopiæ filled
with fruits and ears of corn held in her left, exhibit her as the directress of human events by sea
and land. Nothing can be more dignified than her
noble countenance. As a primary divinity she bears
a diadem on her head, having the person clothed
in a long veil. It is a very remarkable statue for
its excellence of style and its good preservation.
It was found at Ostia.

87. A bust in oriental alabaster bearing erroneously the name of CRISPUS SALLUSTIUS.

88. Lucius Antonius, brother of Marcus Anthony the triumvir. A well sculptured bust.

89. GREEK PHILOSOPHER. A statue.

Before the hemicycle :

90. Lucilla, sister of Traian, draped bust.

91. Marciana, bust. The hair-dress in the form of a diadem.

Passing the column in the following niche :

92. VENUS APHRODITE ANADIOMENA. A statue smaller than life. The goddes of love is here represented in a graceful posture, rising from the sea in the act of arranging and drying her hair. The lower part of this exquisite figure is clothed in drapery of a very elegant style. The marble is the *penthelic*.

93. *See* N.ᵇᵉʳ 27.

94. Hope in Carrara marble removed from the *Quirinal*.

95. Apollo, a statue in greek marble.

Passing the statue of Venus there is an hemicycle adorned with fine columns of a rare black egyptian porphyry found at Sta. Sabina.

Below on the last pillars of egyptian granite;

96. *Julia Mammea*, the wife of Severus, a bust. A. 96. MARCUS ANTONIUS. A characteristic and finely sculptured bust of the celebrated Roman triumvir. It is very interesting as exhibiting the true and iconographic features of the enemy of Cicero.

In the niches round it, are seven statues of athletes, wrestlers, and prize-fighters holding vases

for ointment in their hands. See N^{bers}. 99. 101.
101. 103. 105. 106. *Amongst them there is a remarkable one of an athlete found near the lake
Circeo in the same place where the small statue
of the Faun N.^{r} 41. placed in the opposite niche,
was discovered.*

*On the bracket above stands the bust of
Pius VII, the founder of the present gallery executed by Canova. Round the walls are basreliefs
representing combats between Centaurs and La-
pithæ. — The coloured mosaic of the pavement
represents Diana of Ephesus surrounded by various animals and trees. It was discovered at
Poggio Mirteto in the territory of Sabina in the
year 1801.*

98. Bust of Julia Domna, the wife of Severus.

99. See N.^{ber} 97.

100. Marcus Aurelius the Young. A bust.

A. 100. Bust unknown.

101. See N.^{ber} 97.

102. Cæsar Augustus, a bust.

A. 102. Commodus, bearded bust found at Ostia.

103. See N.^{ber} 97. Found in the Villa of Quintilius Varrus at Tivoli.

104. Veiled bust of a roman lady unknown.

105-106. See N.^{ber} 97.

A. 106. Bust of M. ÆMILIUS LEPIDUS, the
famous triumvir, and the colleague of M. Antonius, and of Julius Cæsar. It was found with
those of M. Antonius and of Cæsar Augustus in a
grotto near *Tor Sapienza,* outside the *Porta Maggiore.*

107. Pallas, a statue in greek marble.

Passing the column:

108. Diana in the chase. Statue in greek marble.

109. THE NILE. A colossal group very valuable for its masterly execution and representation of the admirable symbolic form of this celebrated egyptian river. It is represented majestically leaning against the Sphinx, holding with one hand the cornucopiæ. Graceful little Genii, or Cupids, for the most part restored by the skilful sculptor *Pacetti* surround it; they are embodiments of the sixteen cubits the river rises in its annual overflowing, fertilizing the fruitful soil of Egypt. Some of the Cupids are climbing on the shoulders of the God, others are sporting with ichneumons and crocodiles. It is singular that one of them is represented as rising from the cornucopiae with crossed arms as if to show that the fruitful inundation is completed. As an additional characteristic ornament, we see on the base battles between Tentyrite pigmies, crocodiles, and hippopotami. The lotus-flower appears on the waves with other emblems of Egypt. This classical and majestic group is of Roman workmanship, perhaps a copy from some Greek original, belonging to the best period of the Alexandrian school. It was discovered under the Pontificate of Leo X. near the Church of *Sta. Maria sopra Minerva*, where anciently stood a Serapeium.

110. See N.[ber] 27.

From the hemicycle passing along the gallery, in the first niche:

111. JULIA, the daughter of Titus. A life-size portrait statue sculptured in *Luni* marble found with that of her father Titus on the opposite side, in a garden near the Church of *S. Giovanni del Fonte* at the Lateran in the year 1823. It still retains some traces of the original painting.

Passing the column on the pilaster:

112. JUNO REGINA. A rare and beautiful semicolossal bust adorned with a diadem in the form of a disk, the emblem of the royal dignity and character.

• *Sacrifice of Iphigenia. A basrelief.*

113. Bust of an unknown lady, in flowered alabaster.

114. MINERVA POLYADES OR MEDICEA. A statue. The goddess of wisdom is here represented in a supernatural and dignified character clothed with the majestic peplum negligently thrown over her shoulders, and half-covering the ægis with the left hand, while her right holds a lance, near which a serpent, sacred to her as an emblem of vigilance and health , is coiled. The large mantle falling in rich and multiplied folds to her feet, closely covers the beauty of her form. The helmet adds greatly to the majesty of the head, the outlines of which are of thoroughly severe greek style. The admirable preservation and polish of this statue sculptured in Parian marble, renders it one of the most conspicuous monuments of this Museum. It came from the ruins of a temple on the Esquiline Hill, dedicated, as Publius Victor says, to Minerva Poliades, of which now the ruins alone remain.

115. MAJESTIC BUST UNKNOWN. The band or *laticlavium* across its tunic, is a mark of the senatorial dignity of the personage.

116. Julia, the daughter of Titus, a bust.

117. CLAUDIUS, draped in a well executed toga. A statue worthy of remark for its excellent preservation. Brought here from the Ruspoli Gallery.

· *Triumph of Trajan. The emperor is seen drawn in a chariot guided by Victory.*

118. Colossal head of a SLAVE covered with a cap, found in Trajan's Forum. It evidently belonged to a statue of some barbarian king, subdued by Trajan in one of his victorious conquests. The style of sculpture is beautiful, and shows the fine style, which flourished in the time of that emperor.

119. Bust unknown.

120. FAUNUS resting on the trunk of a tree with a pipe in the right hand. It is worthy of particular notice as a beautiful copy of the famous Faun of Praxiteles.

121. COMMODUS. A rare bust, from Ostia.

122. Bust supposed to be Aurelianus.

123. LUCIUS VERUS. A figure sculptured in the heroic style, representing the colleague of Marcus Aurelius holding in his hand a winged victory on a globe. The short sword or *parazonium* lies at his feet on the folded imperial mantle.

124. PHILIP THE ELDER. A well preserved bust adorned with the girdle of Gabii.

125. Apollo, a bust.

126. *In the niche*: Athlete. Greek statue of a

great value. It was erroneously restored as a Discobolus, a copy from the original of Dorypheros.

127. Bust of a Barbarian prisoner.

128. Bust in egyptian style, with the eyes cnt out.

129. DOMITIAN. The wicked brother of the good Titus is here represented in military costume. This statue larger than life is clothed in the artistically executed paludamentum. It belonged to Giustiniani Gallery.

　*	*Briseis led back to Achilles by Antigonus and Nestor. A basrelief.*

130. Male bust, with the *trabea.*

131. Drusus ? A bust found at Ostia.

132. MERCURY. A statue larger than life. The son of Jupiter and Maïa is dressed with a light pænula, holding the caduceus in his left hand, and standing in the act of receiving with smiling looks the prayers of mortals. The fine dignified countenance, and good execution, render this statue one of the first specimens of greek art. The head , exhibiting much intellectual character, though found in the excavations of the Colosseum, is of the same marble, viz the penthelic, as the whole statue.

133. Julia Domna. Bust.

134. ˙ HEAD OF VESPASIAN. The bust is sculptured in *porta santa* marble, the chlamys being of *verde antico.*

135. HERMES-BUST. A very interesting monument of greek sculpture, in pentelic marble. The inscription in hexameter verses engraved on

its breast deserves the interest of antiquarians. As explained by Winckelman, Visconti, and Nibby, it shows that this hermes anciently exhibited the features of Zeno an African sculptor, who flourished under Antoninus the Pius, and died seventy years old. It stood in the Villa *Negroni* on the Quirinal.

136. * Bust of an old man.

Passing the door of the Library on the left hand, in the middle of the long corridor of inscriptions, we enter this fine Museum by an iron grating adorned on both sides, by two columns of *bigio-lumachellato* marble, with bases of *sassio* marble called *pietra santa* supporting an architrave of white marble.

This magnificent gallery is the work of *Bramante Lazzari* executed during the Pontificate of Julius II, but we are indebted for its modern embellishment to Pius VII whose family name it bears.

Numerous and various monuments both of greek and roman art, collected and purchased by that illustrious Pontiff, from other halls and various excavations, have been here carefully arranged and distributed by *Canova* in two large rows, subdivided into thirty sections, or compartments, each lighted by a large window.

The *Lunettoni* above the upper brackets on the right hand, exhibit some fresco-paintings, whose subjects are allusive to the principal events of the life of Pius VII.

The tasteful arrangement of the monuments of this corridor as well as its astonishing lenght, joined together with the corridor of inscriptions, presents a magnificent view which is terminated by the steps of the *Pio Clementino* Museum, where is an entrance to the garden of the *Pigna*.

In order that Visitors may not have to return to each range, we shall indicate for their greater advantage the choicest monuments both on the right and left of each compartment.

COMP. I. *Passing the iron-grating above to the right, set in the wall:*

1. Pythian Games, celebrated at Athens in honour of Apollo and Bacchus. From the *Lancellotti* palace. A basrelief.

2. Apollo seated. Found in the Colosseum in 1805.

3-4. Scenic masks, actors, and a triumphal pompa or Show.

To the left, fragments set in the wall:

5. Fragment of a basrelief found at *Ostia* representing a headless draped female figure, of very rare greek beauty. Opposite to this, there is that of a male, of which only a leg remains, very finely sculptured.

6. AUTUMN. Recumbent female statue allegorically representing Autumn with the many attributes, which characterise this season as the aries, the hare, the genius of the vintage, a basket of flowers and grapes. It stands on a cover of a sarcophagus exhibiting in relief, the images of a husband and wife with their child, bearing the *bulla*, a medallion, suspended round its breast. It belongs to the time of Adrian, and was discovered on the Cassian way near *Acqua Traversa*.

7-8. The Vintage — Circenses Games.

9-10. Hunting — Venus and Mars — Two fragments, the latter found at *Ostia*.

11-12. Portion of a quadriga — Two Gladiators, a *Retiarius*, and *Mirmillo*.

COMP. II. *To the right:*

13. *Opposite this left side:* WINTER. Another recumbent draped figure representing this season personified with all its various symbols as pine-cones, turtles, little genii playing with swans, a fine exhibition of winter chase. Found at *Ostia* in the year 1805.

14. Euterpe, with the flute. A sitting statue over a cippus dedicated to *Clawtia*.

15-16. Consular statue with the toga, found on the *Appian way* 1818, near the sepulchre of the *Servilii*. — Erato holding the lyre, a statue.

To the left:

17. Faun found in the *Lateran*.

18. Apollo. A statue standing on a *cippus* dedicated to *Caio Octavio Fortunato* and his wife.

19. Paris. A statue on a votive altar to Isis and Serapis.

COMP. III. *Fragments set in the wall:*

20-21. Sileni kneeling, and supporting a basket— Centaur carrying a Cupid.

22-23. Piece of marble ornament — Chase of the Calydonian boar.

24 Covering of a tomb, with Tritons, Nereids, and Isis, referring to the mysteries of this goddess.

25. Head of a bearded man.

26. Head of Septimius Severus.

27. Head of a young Hero.

28-29. Head of Niobe — A Fauness.

30. Bust of Antoninus Pius.

31. Bust unknown.

32-33. Male and Female busts unknown.

34. An altar in the form of a trunk found at Ostia.

35-36. Titus — A Dacian prisoner, bust.

37-38. Fragments of ornament.

39. Altar in *paonazzetto* marble, dedicated to Venus Aphrodite.

40-41-42-43. Fragments of ornaments.

To the left fragments of basrelief set in the wall:

44. A boar hunt.

45. Portion of a sarcophagus with sea-monsters.

46. Bacchus with Centaurs.

47-48. Herma of Bacchus *bifrons* — Female head.

49. Head of Marcus Agrippa.

50-51-52. Bacchante — Germanicus — Faun.

53. Hercules in his boyhood, found at Ostia in 1805.

54-55. Head of a young man — Draped female statue.

56. Bust of Julia Mammaea.

57-58. Gallienus — Alexander Severus, busts.

59. Silenus sitting, a *torso*.

60. Athlete, a bust.

COMP. IV. *Left side, by the grated-door of the New Arm:*

The Attic monuments sent by England. A fresco-painting.
Right side:

61. Urania, a statue removed from the Quirinal.

62. HYGEIA. A statue larger than life. The goddess of health is here represented under the features of an Augusta, probably those of Messalina. The head is adorned with curled hair.

63. Minerva placed on the cippus of *Sextus Cecilius*, a good man,

Left side:

64-65. Heads of Trajan and Augustus placed on the top of the columns on each side of the New Arm.

COMP. V. *Fragments of basreliefs set in the wall*:

66-67-68. Faun — Two Figures — A Bacchante dancing before a Priapus.

69. Sepulchral covering with symbols representing the morning and evening of human life.

· 70. Priest of Bacchus.

71. A conquered province.

72. Cupids at chase.

73. Barbarian captive.

74. A sitting statue of Pluto with Cerberus.

75. Comedian with mask, a bust.

76-77. Female portraits unknown.

78. Apollo crowned with laurel.

79. Dyomedes seized by the hair by the hand of Hercules.

80-81. Ceres — Child's head.

82-83. Mercury — Hygeia with the serpent.

84. Faun playing the flute.

85-86. Beardless Æsculapius with Hygeia. A group.

87. Cupid, or Hercules child found at Tivóli.

88. *Enchased in the wall*: Attributes of Bacchus.

89. The wolf suckling Romulus and Remus.

90. Votive offering in a temple.

91. Meleager in the chase.

92-93-94-95. Genii of Bacchus — Tigers devouring stags — Mercury Psychicompus, or leader of the souls to Hell—Love caressing Psyche.

To the left. Fragments set in the wall:

96. Summer and Autumn personified.

97-98. Sepulchral coverings.

99-100. Cupids with various symbols — The same carrying in triumph the club of Hercules.

101-102. Equestrian figure — Genius of Hercules.

103-104. Two portraits, the first resembling Euripides, the latter unknown.

105-106. Child — Scenic masks.

108-109. Female and male heads unknown.

110. Child amusing himself with a partridge.

111-112-113. Hercules — Venus of Cnidos — Æsculapius with a greek inscription on the plinth. Statues.

114. Child with the toga, holding a volume.

115-116-117-118-119. Bacchante —Funeral feast— Lion's hunting — Cupid in a boat at fish.

COMP. VI. *To the right*:

120. Priestess of Vesta. A statue standing on a cippus sacred to *Caius Valerius*, priest of Serapis. It was discovered on the *Appian Way*.

Excavation of the arch of Costantine and Severus, a fresco-painting.

121. CLIO. A sitting statue of the Muse of history. The guardian of truth is here represented holding a scroll and having on one side volumes and scrolls, bound together in a casket.

122. Diana in the chase.

123. Torse of Diana, over a cippus sacred to the same goddess under the attribute of light-bearer.

124. *Left side* : IMPERIAL PERSONAGE. A statue larger than life, the head bearing a close resemblance to that of Drusus, the brother of Tiberius.

125. Torse of Diana, on a cippus sacred to Mithra s.

COMP. VII. *Fragments of basrelief set in the wall :*

126-127-128. Triton carrying a Nereid — Pastoral scene — The vintage — Æsculapius and Hygeia.

130. The Sun and his worshippers.

131. Icarius and Erigone his daughter.

132-133. Heads unknown.

134. Head of Adonis, found at Tivoli.

135. *On the marble table :* Julius Cæsar veiled as Pontifex Maximus. A head closely resembling the coins of this emperor.

136. Portrait resembling Philippus Junior.

137-138. Two female portraits unknown.

139. Head of a Pancratiast crowned as victor.

140. Herma of a Philosopher found at the Lateran.

141. Hostilianus, a portrait.

142. Hercules *rusticus*. A beardless statue.

143- Unknown male busts.

144-145. Head of the bearded Bacchus, improperly called Plato.

Fragments set lower down in the wall:

146-147. Oxen ploughing.

148. A nest of storks nourished by the parent birds. It is a beautiful allegory of filial love.

Upon the cornice :

149. Another allusive to a sacred subject.

To the left, set in the wall:

150. Death of Perseus for his dislike to the feasts of Bacchus.

151-152-153. Hercules and a Faun — Triumphal Altar — Love and Psyche, the latter is wanting.

154. Pugilistic game on an urn.

155. Sepulchral coffin with the Genius of death.

156. King prisoner, a headless statue.

157. Flavia Domitilla wife of Vespasian.

158-159. Male head —. Head of Domitia.

160-161. Male head — Head representing Lucilla.

162-163-164. Hercules protector of the country — Faun — Male head.

165. Venus Anadyomene, a head.

166-167. Head of an Athlete — Mercury, a figure.

168. Faun carrying a bag-pipe.

169. A Hare running.

170-171-172. Triton with a Cupid — Female figure — A sea monster.

173. FRAGMENT OF A BASRELIEF representing the old Silenus falling from his ass.

Right side :

174. Vine ornament.

COMP. VIII. *Minerva pointing at the restorations to the pictures in the Sale Borgia of the
Library. A fresco-picture.*

175. Bacchus, a ideal figure.

176. NIOBE. A headless and armless statue. As
the action of the figure may relate to many mythological subjects, it is not so easy to determine the
subject which this statue is made to represent.
Diana in the act of descending from her chariot to
contemplate her beloved Endymion, Ariadne in
quest of Theseus on the sea shore, are names
both erroneously attributed to this figure. The
play of the beautiful drapery, naturally agitated
in rich folds by the wind, the action and the mo-
vement of the person, indicate with more probability that of the unhappy Niobe, here represented as turning back her head when in flight from
the arrows of the wrathful Diana.

This very valuable statue was found at A-
drian's villa. It stands on a cippus, on which is
a votive inscription to *Titus Sextius Honoratus*,
dedicated to him by his wife and brother.

177. Polyhymnia. A statue placed on a cippus
referred to *Caius Clodius Amarontis* aged 93 years,
a rare longevity among the Romans.

178. *Left side* : Bacchus, a statue.

179. MITH OF ALCESTIS. A sarcophagus bearing on its cover a latin inscription with the de-
dicacy to *C. I. Evodus* quinquennial chief of the

iron-workers and to *Melilia Acte*, a priestess of Cybele, his wife.

Below, is engraved on basrelief the fabulous story of Alcesta who sacrificed herself for her husband Admetus , a king of Tessaly , celebrated for his misfortunes and piety.

When Apollo had taken refuge at his court, in gratitude for his kind reception, granted him freedom from death, if some one would sacrifice himself instead of him. This touching history is here represented in three different scenes. In the first, on the left, is represented the pilgrimage of Alcestis and her followers to the oracle of Apollo, who is seen standing in the centre of this group, with the tripod, to consult him on the health of Admetus. In the middle the dying Alcestis is represented taking leave of her husband, and her two weeping children Eumelus and Perimela. Lastly to the right, is Pluto in his royal palace with Proserpina. Alcestis covered with a funeral veil turns herself towards her husband Admetus, who is seen brought back from Hell by Hercules. The three Fates look astonished at the event. Her apotheosis is celebrated by the Muses who are surrounding her with scrolls of history and poetry in their hands, to immortalise her name. This large sarcophagus does not deserve great merit for its style, which, is not very good, but it is very interesting in a mythological point of view. The punctures of the eyes and noses of the figures, evidently demonstrate it as belonging to the age of the Antonini. It was discovered at *Ostia.*

1S0. Sepulchral covering from the Quirinal.

181. Diana Triformis, allusive to Heaven, Earth, and Hell.

COMP. IX. *Basreliefs set in the wall:*

182. ALTAR OF GABII exhibiting a very fine representation of Mænades dancing with wild energy around a recumbent Venus, whose hair is raised up by a Cupid. Found in the excavations of the ancient city of *Gabii.*

Upon the cornice, right side:

183. Bacchus entrusted by Minerva to the Nymphs.

184. Sarcophagus with representations allusive to the virtues of the deceased.

185-186-187. Allegory of Peace — Hero on horseback. — Hercules fighting against the Amazons.

188. Head of the young Manilius, crowned.

189-190-191. Sleeping child — Bust of Juno — Boy with two torches, allusive to the morning and evening stars.

192-193-194. Diana — Child smiling.

195. Male torse with chlamys.

A.195-196. Bust of Matidie — Torse of a Faun.

197. PALLAS. Colossal bust of the goddess of war, or as some suppose of Rome personified. The helmet and the torso are not ancient. The eye balls now of email, were perhaps formerly of *pietra gemmaria and ivory,* in order to give to the figure a more natural expression. This highly finished bust is supported by a plinth adorned with heads of oxen, *bucranii,* festoons of flowers, fruits, and birds pecking at them, delicately car-

44

ved. It was found at *Tor Paterno*, the ancient *Laurentum*.

198. Sepulchral cippus representing Romulus and Remus suckled by the wolf.

199-200. Torso of Bacchus - Female head unknown.

A. 200. Torso with chlamys.

201-202. A Reaper — Genius of Summer.

203. Fragment with Etruscan deity.

204. Our Saviour, a basrelief removed from the catacombs, at one time supposed to be a representation of an augur.

205-206. Genii casting the discus — Lion at rest.

207-208-209-210-211. A Standard bearer — Child amusing with a hare — Nereid over a sea monster — Portion of a biga.

Fragments set in the wall, to the left:

212. Matron represented under the attributes of Modesty.

213-214. Bacchic Feasts.

215. Genius of Autamn.

ζ16. Venus seated on a sea-monster.

217-218. Two sarcophagi. On one Venus is represented on a Centaur, on the second some Genii hold a medallion.

219. Bust of Isis, *in pietra di monte*.

220. Roman empress represented as Juno.

221. Antonia Minetes, the wife of Drusus.

222-223. Bust of Jupiter—Head of Julia Mammea.

224. Head resembling Plotina, the wife of Trajan.

225. Half figure of Hercules *rusticus*.

226. Bust supposed to be that of Pythagoras.

227. Bust of an athlete.

228. Terminus, without head.

229. Silenus, herma *bifrons*.

230. Sepulchral cippus dedicated to *Lucio Telesino*.

231. Terminus with a head of Cupid.

232. Bust with head in *nero antico* bearing some resemblance to Scipio Africanus.

233. Bust of Julia Mammea.

234-235-236. Satyr — Oxen ploughing — Genius with burning torch.

237. Woman sitting, representing a conquered province.

238-239. Genius with the horn of plenty — Biga drawn by boars.

COMP. X. *To the right:*

Genius of sculpture pointing to the junction of this corridor, with the *Pio-Clementino* Museum.

To the left:

240. BRITANNICUS, a statue smaller than life representing this unhappy prince, the son of Messalina.

Right side:

241. JUNO SUCKLING A CHILD, perhaps Hercules or Mars, a sitting statue. The dignified character of the figure, and the diadem which adorns the head denotes the Queen of the Gods, and the sister of Jupiter. This group sculptured about life-size was formerly in the Quirinal Gardens. It stands on a bases made in honor of *Flavius Peregrinus Saturninus*, upon which are recorded his various offices and a gilt statue erected to him.

242. Apollo Citharædus, a statue.

Left side:

243. Honorary Cippus to *Marco Aurelio Gregorio* a roman knight.

244. Ocean personified, on a votive altar.

245. Polyhymnia, a statue.

COMP. XI. *Fragments of basreliefs set in the wall, to the right:*

246.247-248. Euterpe and Erato — Melpomenes with Polyhymnia, in company of Homer and Pindarus — Euterpe and Polyhymnia.

250. A votive offering to Apollo, or to Mithras.

251. Cupid and Psyche, a sarcophagus.

252. Torso of Bacchus.

253-254· Vespasian — Niobe.

255-256. Statue of Jupiter Serapis *in bigio* marble — Head of Sappho.

257-258. Bearded head of a prisoner — Statue of Bacchus.

259-260. Unknown male bust — Torse of a Mercury.

261. Female bust unknown.

262. *On the cornices above :* CHILD SMILING, represented in a graceful posture, showing the grapes it holds in the *penula*, the seams of which are to be observed. Found at *Veit* in 1811 with the statue of Tiberius N.ᵇᵉʳ 400.

263-264. Bust resembling Zenobia — Torso of a child.

265. Bust of a greek philosopher.

266-267-268-269. Venus on a Triton — Leg — Hippocampi, or sea horses — A ploughman.

Fragments set above to the left:

270-271. Two Genii — Philosopher holding a scroll.

272. Matron imploring Venus.

273-274. Two sepulchral coverings.

275. Male and female figures.

276. *On the marble table*: Female head unknown.

277. Youthful head resembling the son of Gallienus Saloninus.

278-279. Silvanus — Genius of Sleep, found at *Roma Vecchia* near the Lemonian lake. ·

280-281. Soldier — Male head. unknown.

282-283. Julia Mesa — Hermes of a philosopher.

284-285. Child with birds — Etruscan Bacchus.

286. Silenus, a torse.

A. 286. Statue of a Comedian.

287. *Left side* : A SLEEPING FISHER BOY covered with the *causia*, a fisherman's hat, having a basket under his arm. It came from M.ʳ *Jenkin's* collection.

288-289. Cinerary urns with the image of the deceased.

290-291. Genii of hunting and fishing — Woman giving drink to a boy.

251. A 252. Nymph carried by a Centaur — Genii of the vintage.

COMP. XII. *The fresco painted above in the wall is allusive to the large collection of ancient coins made by Pius VII in the Vatican Library.*

293. Male torso, on the cippus of *Cabrius*.

Right side :

294. HERCULES. A semicolossal statue of the Theban hero, represented in the act of resting after his labours. It was restored by Sig.ʳ *D'Este*

after a model of *Canova*. Found in the territory of *Oriolo* in 1802.

295. Torso of Bacchus.

To the left :

296-297. Victor athlete — Athlete at rest.

298. Statue of Bacchus.

COMP. XIII. *To tho right above, fragments in the wall :*

299-300. Shield with the representation of the battle of Amazons — Portion of a sarcophagus.

301-302. Warrior with a prisoner.

304-305. A Dove couching — A Bull.

306-307 Cinerary urn of a round form — Portion of a vase with a bacchic mask.

308. Child riding on a dolphin.

309-310. A Tiger — Hare eating grapes.

311. A Leopard found at Tivoli in Adrian's Villa.

On the marble-shelves: •

312. FALLEN GLADIATOR , killing a lion , a group. It stands on a plinth of fine alabaster of *Tivoli.*

Left side, set in the wall above :

313-314. Castor with his horse — Fragment of a pastoral scene.

318-319. Mithraic bas relief. — Rustic objects.

320. Genius holding a palm, as a victor.

321-322. A solar quadrant — Bacchanalian procession.

To the left, in the wall above :

323. Mercury preceeding a *quadriga.*

324-325. Two fragments of the chariot races in the Circus.

326. Genii holding a laurel crown.

327-328. Chariot with a child. — Orator on a *quadriga*.

329. A FRAGMENT OF BASRELIEF repre-senting Actœon, surprising Diana in the bath of Gargaphia.

Upon the cornice:

330. Silenus on a chariot drawn by asses.

331-332-333. A bust, and two heads unknown.

334. Medallion with a male bust.

335. Bacchus as a child.

336-337. Bust supposed to represent Getas — Youthful head.

338. Child playing at the *aliossi*.

A. 338-339-340. Faun smiling — Faun with the *pedum* — Genius of winter.

341-342-343. Diana Lucina — Goose catching a fish in the water — Paris.

A. 343. BRUTUS. A life size head of Cæsar's mur-derer.

344-345. Child with apples — Medusa's head.

346. Aristæus the rural god, and the keeper of the herd of the Muses.

347-348. Male figure — Lamp on a tripod.

349-350-351. Fragments with Muses sitting — A cinerary urn with boar's hunting — Love and Psyche.

COMP. XIV. *To the right above:*

A Genius pointing to the Transfiguration, the celebrated oil painting by Raphael. A fresco in the wall.

Right side:

352. VENUS, a handsome litlle statue, standing in a graceful attitude as coming out from the

bath, adorned with a bracelet on her left arm, and bearing a little *balsamarium*, a vase for perfumes to anoint the hair and delicate limbs. The feet and arms have been restored. The monument belongs to · roman workmanship, and shows an extreme beauty of sculpture.

353. Nymph seated on a rock, brought from the Quirinal. It stands over a base dedicated to *Maximianus* the colleague of Diocletian.

354. Venus of Cnidos.

To the left :

355-356. Female figures representing the two Rutiliæ, the Senior and the Younger. Found on the Tusculum.

COMP. XV. *To the right, fragments set in the wall :*

357. Colossal figure of a CAPTIVE KING, sculptured in *frigio* or *paronazzetto* marble. Brought from the Negroni villa.

358-359. Basrelief unknown — Dances.

360-361. Jupiter and Juno in the etruscan style.

362-363. Head of Niobe — Male head unknown.

364-365. Head of Caius Cæsar found at *Ostia*.

366. Faustina the Younger.

367-368. Hercules Victor in the *Pancratiastes* — Female head unknown.

369-370. Bust of Agrippina — Torse belonging to a group of Mars and Venus.

371-372. Female bust — Bust of Sappho.

Right side, upon the cornice :

A.372. A fragment of a basrelief of the eastern frieze of the Parthenon. The equestrian figures represent a portion of the Panathenaic procession.

held in honor of Pallas. This fragment, the only one existing in Italy, was brought from Athens to Venice with the statue of the Cariatid by doge *Morosini*. Afterwards purchased by *'Camuccini* and placed here by Pius VII as a special monument of this Museum. All the sculptured basreliefs which adorned that celebrated temple, the work of Phidias and his pupils, now exist in the *British Museum*.

373-374. Torso of Mars — Male head unknown.

375-376. Griffins.

377-378. Lion with griffins — Stag with a serpent.

Set in the wall to the left:

379-380-381-382. Sepulchral covers with draped figures.

383-384. Annia Faustina, the wife of Elagabalus — Matidie the niece of Trajan.

385-386. Head of Lucilla, the wife of Lucius Verus — Faustina Iunior.

387-388. Male and female heads unknown.

389. Bust of a child.

A.389. Bust of Manilia found on the Appian Way.

390-391-392. Head of Apollo — Trajan — Adrian.

A.392-393. Jupiter — Cupid.

A.393. Bust of Domitia Longina.

394. Bust of Galerius Antoninus found at Ostia.

395-396-397-398. Fragments supporting the cornices, with representations of Tritons and other marine deities.

COMP. XVI. *To the right:*

In the fresco painting above, the Sovereign Pontiff is seen consigning the chyrograph to Ca-

nova, who is here represented as a Genius. This chyrograph alludes to the prohibition to export ancient monuments.

399. Colossal head of Tyberius, found at Veii. It is placed on the honorary Cippus to *Caerellio Politiano.*

400. 494. TYBERIUS. Two sitting semicolossal portrait-statues. The first N.ber 400 exhibits the execrated successor of Augustus at an advanced period of his life, dressed in heroic costume, holding the sceptre and the *parazonium*, a short sword in his hands. The breast is partly covered with a tunic and a civic crown of oak encircles the head. The other, N.ber 494, is also in a sitting majestical posture clothed with the toga, but represented at an earlier period of life. A sum, of 12.000 *scudi* was expended by the Papal Government for the purchase of the latter. They are both remarkable as being of a high style of art, as for their good preservation. The one vas found at *Veii* in 1811, the other at *Piperno*, the ancient *Privernum*, towards the close of the last century.

401. AUGUSTUS, a colossal head found in the excavations of Ostia in 1811.

402. Muse crowned with laurel.

403. Pallas, a statue placed on a Cippus, dedicated to Ceres, *almae frugiferae.—Pax Cererem nutrit — Pacis alumna Ceres.*

COMP. XVII. *Fragments of basreliefs set above to the right:*

404. Mars bound to a tree.

405-406. The four seasons, represented on a sarcophagus.

407-408. The metamorphose of Actæon, changed by Diana into a stag — A *quadriga*.

409-410. Head of a Faun — Head of Ariadne.

411-412. Apollo — A priestess.

413-414-415. Female head unknown — Faun — Venus.

417. THE YOUNG AUGUSTUS. A nearly life size portrait-bust, the best one of all others contained in the present part of the Museum. The emperor is represented in his youth, perhaps in his 14th or 15th year, at the time when coming forth as Cæsar's avenger, he commanded against Anthony the troops, who remained faithful to his adopted father. The noble beauty and style of this bust, its good preservation and the admirable whiteness of the marble, which is *Parian*, are of such walue as to make it superior to all other known imperial busts. It was discovered in the beginning of this century at Ostia in the excavations undertaken by the English consul *Fagan*.

Upon the brackets: Two rare busts of CAIUS and LUCIUS, the two nephews of Augustus, discovered in 1859. near *Sta. Balbina*. The first born of Julia and Agrippa, was adopted by Augustus as his successor.

A. 417. Head of a child, found at *Sta. Balbina*.

418. A draped bust of JULIA the daughter of Augustus. The head-dress reminds us of the fashion of that age, and suites well the character of that princess.

A. 418-419-420. Female head — Head of a child — Flora.

421. DEMOSTHENES. A bust. The physiognomy of the prince of Grecian orators is well expressed in this fine *prothomes*. It came from the *Barberini* collection.

422. Male head unknown.

A. 422. Female head.

423-424. Doubtful head of Cicero — Faun.

To the left:

425-426-427-428-429-430. Fragments set in the wall.

431-432. Male and female heads unknown.

433-434. Head of Horatius — Bust of Silvanus crowned with pine-leaves.

435-436. Bust supposed to be Brutus — A Musa.

437-438. Septimius Severus — Hercules.

439-440. A child weeping — Head of Saloninus.

441-442. Head of Alcibiades — Clodius Albinus.

443-444. Unknown statue — Æsculapius.

445-446. Diana Lucifera — Dyonisiac procession.

447-448. Figures with the *toga* — Minerva.

COMP. XVIII. *To the right above:*

The sculpture personnified by a dignified figure in the act of sculpturing the colossal head of Jupiter, the work of Phidias.

449. Female statue unknown.

450-451. Mercury — Nymph on a votive altar erected by a father for the health of his child.

To the left:

452-453-454. Venus holding a vase of perfumes— Meleager — Æsculapius.

COMP. XIX. *To the right:*

455-456-457. A dying Adonis — Ghariot races —
Death of the children of Niobe.

458-459. A Cow — An Eagle with a Hare.

460. Torso of a harp player.

461-462. Stork — Egyptian Cow.

463-464. Boar in *nero antico* — Mithraic. sacrifice.

465. Swan life-sixe, a good sculpture restored
by *Franzoni*.

466. Phænix. The fabulous bird is in the act of
burning itself on the pire, to rise again from its
ashes.

467. A Dog.

Set in the wall to the left: •

468. Bacchus supported by Ampelus, and Acra-
tus. A bas relief.

469-470-471. A triumphal *pompa·* — Games of
the Circus — Comic scenes.

472-473-474, Female head — Antonia the wife
of Drusus — Faustina the Younger.

475. Male head ornamented with the *tenia*.

476-477-478. Head of Julia Mammea — Domitia — Unknown head.

479-480-481-482. Marble ornaments.

483-484-485. Cupid sleeping — Satiri.

486-487. Two small male *torsi*.

488-489-490-491-492. Fragments of ornaments,

COMP. XX. *To the right*:

*The Tiber personnified, pleased at seeing the
objects of art brought from France to Rome. A
fresco-painting above in the lunetta.*

To the left:

493. DIADUMENIANUS. A statue smaller than life of the son of Opilius Macrinus who was declared Cæsar by his father, and was massacred together with him in a villa of Bitinia, in the sixteenth year of his age.

495. CUPID OF PRAXITELES. A life-sixe statue, one of the best copies of that celebrated original, representing the god in the act of bending his bow. This very elegant figure was found in fragments, and afterwards restored by *Sig.ʳ D'Este*.

497. PRISTINUM. Fragment of a large sarcophagus representing a corn-mill turned by horses. The mill pertains to the species of the *trusatiles jumentariae*. The sculpture belongs to the period of the decay of art. It was found in the year 1836, outside the modern gate of *S. Giovanni*.

A. 497. *Above:* Basrelief belonging to the age of the Antonini, representing children playing with walnuts, a game now known under the name of *castelletto*. Discovered on the *Via Appia* in the A-*mentola* vineyard.

Above to the right, on the marble-shelf:

498. Clotho one of the *Parcae*, found at Tivoli in Adrian's Villa.

COMP. XXI. *Set in the wall to the right:*

499-500-501. Fragments of sarcophagi.

502. Female head larger than life.

503-504. Youthful head unknown — A child of Niobe.

505. Head of Antoninus Pius with the civic crown.

506-507. Heads of Athletes.

508. HEAD OF AN ORATOR. A very expressive

and well sculptnred head represented in the act of
haranguing the people.

509-512. ARIADNE AND VENUS — Among the
fine heads of this collection, these are worthy of
particular remark. The one of Ariadne, larger
than life, exhibits features expressive of great,
though mournful beauty. The other shows us one
of the most elegant, and graceful representations
of ideal beauty. Its admirable preservation, and
the particular and elegant arrangement of the hair, makes it one of the best heads, that has come
down to us. It is of the well known kind of marble
called *Greco duro*, and was discovered in 1804
in front of the Baths of Diocletian.

A. 510. CATO. This fine head well expresses the
severity of that celebrated roman called by Cicero
« the father of his country » It stands on a lion's
paw, and came from the *Randanini' s* collection.

511. C. MARIUS. A bust. The proud consul appears here, as we may suppose, looking sternly
at the Cymbrian slave sent to murder him, and
terrifying him with the well known words: « Hast
thou, Barbarian, the courage te kill Caius Marius ! ! » It stands on a base like that of Cato.

Left side, on the cornice above :

513. Female head unknown —

A. 513. Venus.

514-515. Cupid and Psyche — Fragment of ornament.

516. Bacchante dancing.

Left hand, above :

517-518-519. Nymph on a sea monster — Fragments of sarcophagi.

520-521. Fragment of a sarcophagus, in which a devotee of Juno was buried — The Autumn symbolised by a Genius.

522-523. Cupid and Psyche — Jupiter Ammon.

524-525. Head of Hercules *Rusticus* — Head of Plautilla.

526-527. Faun crowned with ivy — Head of a roman orator.

528-529. Herma of an Indian Bacchus.

530. Livia Augusta.

531. Phocion. Helmeted head like the one standing in the Hall of the *Biga* in the *Pio-Clementino Museum.*

532-533. Bust of Diana — Sarcophagus with the figure of the deceased represented.

534-535. Bust of Juno *Persiphonia* — Philoctetes expressing his sorrow for the bite of the serpent sent by Juno.

A. 535. Head of Claudius.

536. Athlete.

537-638-539-540. Fragments of basreliefs : An emperor at chase — A Bull — Chariot drawn by rams — Ox resting.

541-542. Animals feeding — Equestrian figure.

COMP. XXII. *To the right, above :*

Architecture represented by a female figure, which amidst the fragments of ancient art, is pointing to the Nuovo Braccio.

543. Cuirass with Romulus and Remus sculptured.

544. SILENUS. A statue. In this beautiful monument of Greek workmanship, we see a good representation of the companion of Bacchus. With

one hand, he presents in a small cup a libation to
a lynx or panther, which gazes on him, whilst
with the other has risen on his head the thyrsus
or pastoral crook, as admonishing it. The only
restorations of this valuable statue, sculptured in
salino marble, are the legs in the lower part. It
was discovered in 1791 near the *Aricia* in a villa
which anciently belonged to *Mummius Regulus*,
a member of the college of the *Arcales*. It is placed on a base erected in honour of *Titus Arru-
tenius*, by his friend *Anicius Glabrius*.

545. Cuirass with the head of Drusus.

546. *Left side:* SABINA. A statue well described by Visconti, representing the wife of Adrian,
standing as Venus with an apple in her hand. The
texture of the drapery is so light and so admirably arranged, as to leave the beautiful forms of
her body, perfectly visible beneath it. It formerly
stood in the *Pio-Clementino Museum.*

547. ISIS. A colossal bust. It was long supposed that this fine monument of greek workmanship, represented Cybele, the mother of all the
Gods, but the lotus flower, one of the principal
characteristics of the Goddess, worshipped by the
Egyptians as the giver of fertility, removes all
doubt on the subject, and clearly demonstrates it
to represent Isis. An ample veil covers the head,
and the neck is adorned with many necklaces
formed of acorns. This imposing monument sculptured in penthelic marble stands on a cippus
enriched with some hexameter verses, with muses grouped around a poet, playing on the lyre,

and trees sacred to Apollo. It was brought here from the Gardens of the *Quirinal.*

Right side :

548. Statue of Diana Lucifera, placed on the cippus of *Papinia Incomparabili Fœminarum.*

COMP. XXIII. *Fragments set in the wall to the right:*

549. Woman making a votive offer to Æsculapius.

550. A representation of the *Ludi Castrenses.*
A.550. A large rectangular slab, ornamented with animals and figures of gods. A Medusa's mask decorates the argolic shield which fills the middle. It is admirable for its finish of execution and skill of sculpture. It perhaps alludes to the " *Castrenses ludi* " gymnastic exercises of the camp.

551. Epicurus meditating.

552-553-554-555. Male and female heads — Antoninus Pius — Pompey — Lucius Verus in his youth.

556-557. A Child of Niobe — Pallas.

558. BACCHUS WITH AMPELUS. Colossal group. A chaplet of ivy and grapes, encircles the head of the God. He leans towards his young companion, looking at him with a smiling countenance, and holds a cup in the left hand, which is thrown over the shoulders of Ampelus.

559-560. Annius Verus — Trajan.

561. Bust of Domitius Enobarbus on a cippus dedicated to *Julia Epanthaea.*

562-563. Male bust wearing the chlamys — Aristotle

564-565. Woman sitting — Hercules in repose.

566. Ceremony in honor of Bacchus, or of Ceres.

To the left, fragments set in the wall:

567. The Genius of evil, an egyptian deity found at Ostia — By some it is supposed to be an allegorical personification of Time.

568. Sacrifice to Mithras, with Genii representing the Moon and the Sun. Found at Ostia.

On the marble table:

669-570-571. Unknown female heads — Head of Juno.

572-573-574. Unknown male heads — Trajan,

575-576. Antonia the wife of Drusus — Julia the daughter of Titus.

577-578-579. Small male torso — Silenus — Mercury.

580. *Left side, on the cornice:* Small statue of a PREFICA, one of those hired female mourners, who wailed over the corpse at funeral rites, weeping, with disheveled hair, and beating their breasts. Found on the Pincian Hill in 1827.

581-582-583. Torso of Hercules — Faun — Silenus.

584-585-586. Fragments of pilasters with carvings.

COMP. XXIV. *The Academy of St. Luke's instituted for the benefit of the three Arts sisters: Painting, Sculpture and Architecture — A fresco painting.*

587. Faustina the Elder, under the attributes of Ceres, standing on a cippus to *Athenadoro Annonae Praefecto.*

To the left:

588. VENUS GABINA. A statue found at *Gabium*.

589. MERCURY, an elegant statue, the head covered with the petasus. In his hand he holds the caduceus, and the purse. Found near the *Monte di Pietà*.

Upon the cornice:

590. Torso of Bacchus on a cippus sacred to Apollo.

591. Claudius, with the head of Augustus. The cippus on which it stands bears the inscription to the Sun : *Numini Invicto Soli Mithrae.*

592. Torso of Apollo, *Cœlispex,* wearing a band on which the signs of the Zodiac are represented. Found in the theatre of *Valle* in 1820.

COMP. XXV. *Fragments set in the wall to the right :*

593-594. A religious procession — Votive fragment with the family represented.

595-596. Bacchanalian feast — Bacchus and Ariadne attended by Cupids.

597-598. Bust of a child — Carneades the philosopher.

599-600-601. Paris — Augustus — Manlia Scantilla.

602-603. Male bust unknown — Child smiling.

A.603-604. Bacchus disguised as a Venus — Faun.

605-606. Head crowned with pine leaves—Genius.

Upon the cornice:

A.606. NEPTUNE. A well preserved and splendidly sculptured head in penthelic marble.

607. A Genius.

A.607. Bust unknown.

608-609. Agrippina Junior — Torso of Diana.

610-611-612-613. *Fragments set down the wall:*
Triton with a Nereid — Reapers — Chariot-races
in the Circus. — Genii of Summer and Winter.

Fragments set above to the left side:

614-615. A barbarian — Front of a cippus.

616-617. Ornaments with griffins — Death of
Meleager.

618-619. Marcus Brutus — Agrippina the Elder.

620-621. Head unknown — Tiphon, an egyptian
deity.

622-623-624. Faustina the Younger — Domitia —
Trajan Youthful.

Upon the cornices:

625. Antinous.

A.625. Faun.

626. Head of Isis.

A.626. Torso of a Child.

627. Venus and Mars, a group.

628. Torso supposed to be an Hercules.

A.628. Head of the Young Augustus.

629. Male bust unknown.

A.629. Female head with a veil.

630-631-632-633-634. Fragments of ornaments of
sarcophagi.

COMP. XXVI. *To the right hand on the wall:*
*The Public Walk of the Pincian Hill. A fre-
sco-painting.*

635. Torso with head of Phillip the Younger,
standing on a sepulchral cover.

636. *Right side:* HERCULES WITH TELE-
PHUS *or* AIAX IN HIS ARMS. A highly fini-
shed-statue, one of the finest which adorn this Mu-

seum. It clearly shows the difference between the greek and roman taste of sculpture. The hair is dressed in a round form, well agreeing with the character of the whole figure, the beauty of which, is principally to be admired in the head and legs. Found under *Julius II.* in the *Piazza di Campo di Fiori*, near the theatre of Pompey.

637. Torso of some imperial personage.

To the left hand :

638. Hermaphroditus, a mutilated statue.

639. JULIA SOEMIA, the mother of Elagabalus standing seminude as Venus. Her head is dressed with a moveable wig. It was discovered in the *Forum* of *Praeneste.*

640. Male torso unknown.

COMP. XXVII. *Fragments put along the lateral walls.*

641. JUNO AND THETYS. A very rare and interesting fragment of basrelief. It represents Juno *Pronuba,* or the goddess of marriages and births, in the act of persuading Thetys, the goddes of the sea, to marry Peleus, a hero of Thessaly, and the father of Achilles. This marriage was the only one wich was celebrated between a mortal and an immortal. The goddess is represented seated on a rock in a pensive attitude, while Juno is raising the veil from her head.

642-643. FRAGMENTS OF BASRELIEF in pentelic marble of excellent style the one representing Bacchus intrusted to the Nymphs, the other a small figure of a woman turned backwards, in the act of hanging on the *tholus,* or interior dome of a temple, a votive offering.

644. FRAGMENT OF A BASRELIEF, representing a bacchanalian festival, with Mænades
dancing and pouring out wine. The marble is the
pentelic. It, was discovered on the Esquiline in the
Villa Palombara.

645. Celebration of the mysteries of Bacchus.

646-647. An Athlete — Atys, a priest of. Cybele.

648. Apollo Lycius, found at the *Aquae Albulae*
near Tivoli.

649-650. Cupid — Bacchus.

651. Child pressing a swan to its breast. A fine
allegorical representation of Winter.

652. *On the bracket*: CENTAUR. Beautiful head
in greek marble.

Set in the wall above, to the left hand :

653. Winged Cupid.

A.653. Antonia the sister of Augustus.

654. Isis found at Tivoli.

655. Perseus shewing the head of Medusa, he
has just cut off, to the daughter of Cepheus. A
group.

656. Torso of Bacchus.

657-658-659-660. Fragments of pilasters and sarcophagi, with figures of griffins, birds etc.

Fragments of basreliefs in the wall :

661-662-663. A poet — Venus and Mars — A
tragic poet.

664-665-666. Child unknown — Juno — Æsculapius.

667-668-669. Glaucus — Jupiter Serapis — Daughter of Niobe.

670-671. Head unknown of a child —The Young
Hercules.

5

A.671. Herma of Bacchus.

672. Ganymede with the eagle.

A.672. Male bust unknown.

673. Venus crowned by Genii with flowers.

A.673-674. Head of Phillip the Younger — Ganymede.

A.674..Herma of Bacchus.

675-676-677. Statue of Bacchus — Fragments of marble ornaments.

678. Sarcophagus representing the Genius of the sea.

679-680. Fragments of ornaments.

COMP. XXVIII. *To the right:*

The Memory of the Arazzi or Tapestries drawn by Raphael stolen in 1798, and afterwards recovered at Leghorn from a Jew, with their settlement in the place where now they are to be found.

681. Pallas, a statue.

682. ANTONINUS PIUS. A heroic semicolossal statue representing the good emperor clothed in a military dress, holding the *parazonium*. It was found at *Tivoli* in Adrian's villa.

683. Hygeia.

To the left:

684. Æsculapius, on a votive altar to the same God.

685. *Left side:* LARGE SARCOPHAGUS in marble of Luni. As we may see from its inscription, it belonged to a certain *Nonius Asprenatus*. It was found ·in a villa belonging to him. It is worthy of interest on account of its representation of the different operations of making oil, and

grinding olives. It also exhibits the names of five
liberti, all bearing the surname of their family,
and of their profession of oil merchants. On the
left side are sculptured various instruments used
in their profession and some measures, as the
quartarius, sextarius, the *hemina* etc.

686. TUCCIA. A statue, representing this vestal virgin, in the act of carrying water from the
Tiber to the temple of Vesta in a sieve, to prove
her chastity. Her countenance reveals an expression of modesty, mingled with assured ingenuity.
On the border of the sieve there are three letters
viz S. K. P. which means : " By this proof a
sepulchre and a calumny are removed from me " .

COMP. XXIX. *To the right, fragments set in
the wall* :

687· Death of Clitemnestra.

688. Menelaüs snpporting the corpse of Patroclus.

689. A military funeral procession.

690. The ramson of the body of Hector.

691-692. Head of a Bacchante — Head resembling Matidie.

693. *Right side, on the shelf :* THE YOUTHFUL
HERCULES. Colossal head crowned with a wreath
of poplar leaves. This beautiful head is one of the
best specimens of greek chisel, in *grechetto* marble. It came from *Aldobrandini's Gallery*.

694-695. Juno with diadem — Head of one of
the Dioscuri.

696-697. Head of Plotina — Female head unknown.

698. *On the bracket* : CICERO, A fine, and well preserved bust, supposed to be that of the Prince of Roman orators. It was discovered at *Roma Vecchia*, beyond the tomb of *Cecilia Metella*, in the *Lemonium*, anciently the villa of the Brothers *Quintilii*, afterwards confiscated by Commodus.

A.698-699. Quintus Erennius — Child.

A.699.-700. Antonia the wife of Drusus Senior — Antoninus Pius, found at Ostia.

A.700. Annius Verus.

701, ULYSSES, offering a libation to the giant Polyphemus; a very expressive little statue. The hero is dressed in a seaman's garb, covered with the phrygian bonnet on the head.

Set in the wall above, to the left side:

A.701-702. Faustina Junior — Commodus represented in his youth.

703-704-705-706-707. Fragments of ornaments set down the cornices in the wall.

Fragments set in the wall to the left:

708. Dancing Faun.

709. A BASRELIEF, in which Bacchus is seen riding on a tiger, followed by Silenus standing on an ass, and by the merry followers of the god, Fauns and Bacchantes.

Below, under the shelf of marble:

710. Fauns.

711-712-713. Julia Pia — Bust of Sabina — Melpomenes.

714-715-716. Ariadne — Child — Female head.

717. Head of Julianus the Apostate.

718-719. Faun sculptured in green *basalte* — Herma of Carecades.

220. Herma *bifrons* of Jupiter in penthelic marble.

721-722-723. Busts of Manilia Ellas — Manilius — Manilius Faustus. They were found on the Appian Way by St. Sebastian in the sepulchre of their family.

724. Herma of Bacchus in *giallo antico* styled *carnagione*. Found on the Pinclan.

725-726. Male head and torso unknown, in basalte.

727-728-729. Fragments of basreliefs, and architectural ornaments.

COMP. XXX. *The colossal Spur erected by Pius VII. for the preservation of the northern portion of the Flavian Amphitheatre under the direction of Cav. Valadier — A fresco painting.*

730. PENELOPES. A mutilated draped figure supposed by Thiersch to be Penelope, from its strong resemblance to the one that stands in the Gallery of Statues in the *Pio-Clementino Museum.* The style of the sculpture closely resembles the etruscan.

Opposite the entrance to the Giardino della Pigna.

731. Herma of a Philosopher.

732. HERCULES. A semicolossal recumbent statue. It formerly stood in the *Villa d'Este* at *Tivoli.*

733. *To the left:* Herma of Solon with the name written in greek characters.

THE PIO-CLEMENTINO MUSEUM.

Having reached the end of the *Chiaramonti Museum*, we ascend the marble steps which lead to the vestibule of this important department of the Vatican, and enter it by a rich and elegant iron grating.

This large building was erected by the Pontifs Julius II. Innocent VIII and Leo X ; but Clement XII. and Pius VII whose immortal names this portion of the Museum bears, greatly enlarged it by the construction of various magnificent galleries. The latter were adorned by their good taste with fine specimens and masterpieces of art, which formerly were scattered over other particular collections, purchased at their own expense.

SQUARE VESTIBULE OF THE BELVEDERE

So called from the beautiful view it commands of Rome. The cieling is adorned with stuccoes and frescoes on scriptural subjects by *Pierin del Vaga* and by *Ricciarelli*, or *Daniele da Volterra*, both a painter and sculptor, a friend of *Buonarroti*.

Beginning on the right hand, the monuments are arranged as follows:

1. ROMAN LADY reclining as Venus on a convivial couch. Two little Cupids stand at her head, the one offering her a mortuary crown, the other

holding a quiver. This monument, purchased by Clement XIV. from the *Giustiniani* gallery, stands in the same place, where during the time of Julius II. stood the statue of Ariadne, erroneously called Cleopatra, which now may be seen in the Gallery of Statues

In the middle of the vestibule:

2. *Opposite this torso :* SARCOPHAGUS *in peperino* or grey-vulcanic *tufa* ornamented with roses and triglyphs in the doric style. This important monument may be referred to the time of the Republic. It is dedicated to *L. Cornelius Scipio Barbatus,* great grand father of *Scipio Africanus,* who was consul in the year of Rome 456. According to the Latin inscription, he was of noble birth, a wise and potent man, he had been Censor, and Ædile, took the provinces of *Samnium,* and *Taurasia,* subjugated all *Lucania* and led away some hostages. The style of the inscription is primitive, in the so called *Saturnian* number, viz in a rough and imperfect verse. Over the sarcophagus is the bust of a young man crowned with laurel. Probably it belongs to a member of the Scipio family, perhaps representing *Ennius,* or *Scipio* the son of *Gnaeus.* When this interesting monument was discovered in the tomb of the Scipios, on the Appian way, an entire skeleton of a man was found within, with a ring on the ring-finger. The bones were removed to *Padua* by *Quirini,* and the ring was given by Pius VI to the antiquarian *Dulens,* and is now preserved in the collection of the *Earl* of *Beverley,* whose family has since been raised to the Duke-

. dom of Northumberland. Lining the walls are several other inscriptions, relative to the various
members of the Scipio, and Cornelii families.
Amongst them, one especially to the marked, records the name of Publius Cornelius Scipio. It is
to be found in the inscription of the sarcophagus beneath. Some are of the greatest antiquity,
and all were found in the same place as the sarcophagus, viz in the *Vigna Sassi* near *Porta Ca-
pena* in the sepulchre of the family, which was
discovered in the year 1780.

*Passing under the arch of this vestibule we
enter the :*

ROUND VESTIBULE

It is formed of four square niches. The ceiling is ornamented with a *chiaroscuro* by *Unterperger* representing the Church delivering to Rome the *tiara* or Papal diadem.

3. THE TORSO BELVEDERE. In this splendid
fragment of antiquity, the more celebrated antiquarians, amongst which *Winckelmann*, and *Mengs*
the painter, have recognised *Hercules* as deified,
and admitted into the company of the Gods. Indeed
the softness of the form, the absense of veins and
nerves, and the muscles rising without tension,
or rigidity, plainly show the absense of mortal
blood, and earthly wants, as is natural in a spi-
rited body, elevated above human nature, and
nourished with the heavenly nectar. This torso
was highly esteemed both by *Raphael,* and *Michael Angelo,* who took it as a model for their

studies. The latter also took a model of it, which he preserved at *Florence*, with the intention of perfecting it, according to the original form, but death prevented him from carrying out his design. In that model *Michael Angelo* represented Hercules as reposing after his labours, and standing in company with Hebe, his celestial bride. Some consider with *Visconti*, that the right hand was resting over the head, or rather holding the cup of immortality, others, and among them *Winckelmann*, consider it as extended for the purpose of caressing Hebe, whose figure is supposed to stand at his left side. This torso is the most beautiful known, and as regards grandeur, it excells all other antique statues. So great is the resemblance it bears to human flesh, that the eye almost fails to detect the difference, and this is especially to be remarked in the sides. Its fame is such, as to render it worthy of the man who sculptured Patroclus sustaining *Menelaus*, a group better known under the name of *Pasquino*. It is the work of Apollonius son of Nestor of Athens, as the greek inscription on the base indicates. From the name of the artist, we may infer its date to be later than the time of Alexander the Great. The marble is the penthelic. It was found towards the end of the fifteenth century in the *Campo di Fiori*, where anciently stood the magnificent theatre and *Portico* of Pompey.

4-5. TWO FRAGMENTS of male figures, both remarkable for the fine arrangement of their drapery: N.ᵇᵉʳ 4. bears the greek sandals. N.ᵇᵉʳ 5. was greatly admired and studied by Raphael, for the beauty of its drapery. Both are of a high class of greek sculpture. The former was found at *Castrum Novum* near *Civilavecchia;* the latter outside the *Porta Portese,* along the Tiber. On a cippus there is an inscription to *Catus Julius Cæsar.*

6. *Above in the wall:* BASRELIEF, on which are represented Cupid and Psyche before Pluto and Proserpina, who are seated on their thrones as they vere graphically described by *Apuleius* in his fables. Found at *Ostia.*

In front of this vestibule and overlooking a portion of the Vatican Gardens is the balcony called:

LOGGIA DEL BELVEDERE. *If received its name from the beautiful view, it commands of the principal monuments of the City, the Campagna, and the distant Alban, Latin, and Tusculan Hills, the Sabine, and Volscian mountains, and the lower Apennines.*

On this balcony is : A VERY RARE ANE-MOSCOPIUM, or ancient compass, on the twelve sides of which are inscribed the greek and latin names of the winds, and the four principal divisions of the heaven. It is very interesting being the best one known of its kind, and was discovered on the Esquiline, near the *Colosseum* in 1779.

7-8. FRAGMENT of a female figure which has the feet crossed. Its style is excellent — The lower part of a figure, which holds the *cornucopiae.* Found at *Roma Vecchia.*

9. The large BASIN *of paronazzetto* which stands in the centre of this vestibule, measures twenty five palms in circumference. It was found

76

in the *Val d'Inferno* beyon1 *Porta Angelica*. It was placed here after its removal from the *Sale Borgia* in the Library.

At the four angles of this vestibule there are:

ROOM OF THE MELEAGER

10. So called from the celebrated statue standing in the centre. The hero of Calydonia, the subject of so many fables of both Greek and Latin poets, although deficient of the left arm, may be here admired in all the splendour of physical beauty. He is represented in a noble attitude resting on his lance, which is here wanting, holding with the left hand the head of the boar. His faithful dog stands at his feet, on the right side. The countenanne of the young hero is very fine and wonderfully expresses the satisfaction he feels, at having slain the monster. The elegant drapery scarcely covers the breast, and passing over the shoulders, is twisted round his left forearm. This highly finished statue is sculptured in *tinezio* marble, and it is perhaps a copy after the greek paintings of *Polignotus, and Possolasius*. It served as precious object of study to the great artists of the sixteenth century. It is even said, that Michael Angelo did not restore it, on account of its sublime beauty. It came from the Caesarian Gardens, outside *Porta Portese*.

11. Fragment of a statùe covered with a net, found at Tivoli in Hadrian's villa.

12. Male torso on a cippus sacred to *F. Claudio Oreste*.

13. *Above*: Basrelief with the Muses represented.

- 14-15-16. Bust unknown—Altar with inscription to *Atimeto Gnaeo Cornelio* — Plato.

17. *On the wall above:* An interesting *inscription* engraved on tiburtine stone in Latin characters. It relates to the foundation and dedication of a temple, to *Herculi Victori* in Rome, by the consul *Mummius* the conqueror of Corinth, to fulfil a vow, made by him in the war of Achaïa. Though imperfect in form, it is of high importance in an historical and archeological point of view, being but little inferior, to that of the sepulchre of the Scipios.

18-19. Unknown statue — Torso unknown.

20. Basrelief with representation of a sea-port.

21. TRAJAN, a colossal bust.

Below, to the left side :

22. A Roman votive *biremes*, or galley of two tiers of oars, very elegantly executed. On the stern poop is the image of Pallas, the tutelary deity of the ship, and the crocodile, a symbol of Egypt. It has been supposed that it represented a part of the Flagship, « The Alexander » Mark Antony's vessel at the battle of Actium, or better a votive offering hung on some temple of Fortune. Found at *Palestrina;* the ancient *Praeneste.*

23-24. Male torsi — Fragments of a vase in *basalte.*

Reentering the round vestibule, we proceed on the right hand to the :

OCTANGULAR COURT OF THE
BELVEDERE

Built after the design of *Bramante*, the porch erected after that of *Simonelli*, under Clement XIV. It is supported by sixteen fine columns of *breccia corallina*, *bigio*, and white marble, with capitals of *serpentino* green, red porphyry, and *giallo antico*, which formerly were in the *Sale Borgia* now a portion of the Vatican Library. The exterior and interior walls of this court are decorated with urns, baths, basreliefs, columns, sarcophagi, medallions, and statues, some of which, however, much neglected. In the cabinets, at the four corners of the court, we admire some of the most celebrated monuments of art, such as the Apollo of Belvedere, Mercury, the Laocoon etc.

The eight large medallions, and masks placed round the court, were brought here from the baths of Agrippa.

Beginning on the right hand round the porch, at the side of the entrance:

25. Fine column of a very rare granite called "*Morrighone*" found at Palestrina.

26. Column of white marble with festoons, found at Tivoli.

27. Foot of a table or *Triclinium* with griffins, a basrelief found in the Villa Negroni on the Viminal.

28. A LARGE OVAL SARCOPHAGUS found in 1772 in laying the foundations of the Sacristy

of St. Peter's, on the spot where anciently stood
the Circus of Nero. Two skeletons were found in
it. The beautiful figures which are sculptured in
basrelief over its sides, represent a solemn celebration of the Bacchic orgies, by dancing Fauns
and Bacchantes. The latter are remarkable for
their dishevelled hair, and the energetic movements of their bodies, produced by the violent
action of dancing. Some are playing on the tam-
bourins, *tympana* and *crotala* , one holds the mystic cradle of Bacchus, another brandishes the
thyrsus, adorned with pine-cones. Two colossal
heads of lions in *alto rilievo* skilfully executed,
stand at each end of the sarcophagus, and add no
little to the grandeur of the whole.

29. *Opposite this :* BATH of fine black egyptian
basalte, but more probably of some volcanic composition. Found in the *Thermae of Caracalla*.

30. Nymph sleeping. Found outside the *Porta
Latina*.

31. SEPULCHRAL COFFIN in white marble.
It is very interesting for its *Greek-Latin* inscription, which proves it to be the sepulchre of
Sextus Varius Marcellus, the father of the Emperor Elagabalus. It enumerates his various offices and dignities, such as that of Procurator of
the waters, procurator of the province of Brittany,
Procurator of the private treasury of the Emperor, mentionning also the honorary of 100, 200,
and 300 sextertii, according to the various offices,
with which he was invested. Found at *Velletri*.

So styled from the three fine statues it contains, the work of that eminent artist, the prince
of modern sculptors, viz, the *Perseus*, and the
two *Pugilists*, or Boxers.

32. PERSEUS is represented as holding in his
right hand the *harpe* or curved sword, given
him by Mercury, for the purpose of cutting off
the viperous head of Medusa, which he is raising
up with his left. The mantle falls down from his
shoulders in rich folds, aud reaches to his feet.
The idea expressed in this excellent piece of sculpture is very dignifying, and exquisitely predo-
minates over the form, which shows such wonderful beauty, delicacy, and skill in art, as to make
it worthy of the perfection of the happy times of
Athens. It formerly stood in the place of the Apollo,
when the latter vas carried off to Paris by the
French Government.

33-34. The two pugilists * GREUGAS AND
DAMOXENUS are statues remarkable for their
athletic forms, and the attitudes appropriate to
their profession of boxers. Greugas raises his arm,
and presents his undefended side to Damoxenus
his assaillant, whose cruel and fiercy look, and
the extended fingers of his right hand, admirably
express his treachery, and his utter disregard for
the laws prescribed in the games , a tale which
Pausanias so well relates in the XX. chapter of

* Creugas was born at Dyrrachium, the latter to Syracuse.

his description of Acadia. Pius VI. purchased these statues, and to do honor to the great sculptor, caused them to stand by the best masterpieces of antiquity.

A. 34. MERCURY AGOREUS FORENSIS, so called from the Forum, or place of trade, where it anciently stood, and where he presided as a god of eloquence, or, of merchandise. Amongst the other emblems, it bears the *caduceum*, and is remarkable for its form and preservation. Found at *Praeneste*.

Opposite this:

35. Minerva, found by the temple of Peace.

Outside the Cabinet:

36. Basin of black egyptian granite found in the Circus of Nero.

37. ARIADNE found by Bacchus in the island of Naxos. A valuable basrelief sculptured on an ancient sarcophagus, discovered at *Orte in 1823.*

39. *Above to the wall:* LARGE BASRELIEF representing Ceres and Diana, combating against the Titans, and a Giant. The Titans stand on the top of the mountain, in the act of hurling stones at Ceres, who with a torch in each hand, advances to meet them, while Diana with her bow, shoots an arrow at the Giant, represented under the form of a monster half man, half serpent. This interesting frieze sculptured in Carrara marble, was found in the *Villa Mattei.*

39. TRIUMPHAL POMPA, celebrated by some roman consul, or proconsul. It is sculptured on a large sepulchral coffin, which for its style may be referred to the times of Adrian. On its cover are

6

represented the four seasons. Discovered outside the Flaminiam Gate.

40. COLUMN of a very rare *breccia affricana corallina*.

41. Portion of a cornice in *rosso antico* standing on a basis erected to *Onestus Caestus Athictus*. Found at Veii, at present known under the name of *Isola Farnese* ten miles far from Rome.

42. Cippus dedicated to *Veratia Prisca*.

43. *In the niche:* SALLUSTIA BARBIA ORBIANA, wife of Alexander Severus, standing as Venus with an apple in her hand, and a Cupid as her left side. This statue, remarkable for the good style of art, was dedicated to the same Empress by two of her freed-women *Helpidia* and *Sallustia*, as the inscription in the plinth shows. Found near *Sta. Croce in Gerusalemme* in the villa, which formerly belonged to Alexander Severus.

Below is a large bath of rare *rosa* alabaster.

44. ALTAR bearing the inscription of Tyberius Claudius Faventinus, dedicated to Mars and Venus. It exhibits various mythological subjects allusive to these deities, as the judgment of Paris, the body of Hector dragged behind the car of Achilles around the walls of Troy, the Vestal Rhea Silvia in the wood, and Romulus and Remus suckled by the she-wolf. It was found on the Celian Hill in the *Millini* gardens.

45. THE ALTAR, below the former, of an oblong form is sculptured in pentelic marble in excellent style, though much damaged by time. It is called the *Lararium* of Augustus, from the principal exploits of this emperor, which it exhibits

on its four sides. On the first we see the *Lara-rium* or place consecrated to the house-hold gods, in which are some sacred utensils, together with the veiled figures of Augustus, Livia his wife, Octavia, and his mother, who followed by her grand-children, presents to him the images of the house-hold Gods. On the other side, there is a half effaced Latin inscription supported by a winged figure of Victory, and dedicated to Augustus by the Roman Senate and People. The third side exhibits Latinus, the founder of the *Gens Julia*, from whom the emperor descended. He is represented as seated near the Laurentine wood, holding in his hand a volume, in allusion to his alliance with Æneas. The figure of the latter is seen standing by, witth the sow, relative to his marriage with Lavinia. Lastly on the fourth side, Augustus may be seen led to the Empyreal region, in a chariot drawn by two winged horses, and in the act of being received by his adopted father Julius Cæsar, a part of whose figure is still visible among the clouds. In the lower part of this side are Livia, his two adopted sons Tiberius and Drusus as Cupids, and the figure of Rome personified, bidding him a last farewell. This interesting basrelief was discovered on the Palatine Hill. Undoubtedly it is of the time of this Emperor.

46. Portion of a cornice in *rosso antico* with a cippus sacred to *Tiberio Claudio Polideuce.*

Opposite this:

47. Cippus with latin inscription.

48. Front of a sarcophagus with the images of the husbands assisted by Melpomene, Thalia, Clio, and Euterpe. A basrelief.

49. LARGE SARCOPHAGUS in *alto rilievo*, exhibiting a combat between the Amazons and the Greeks. Some of the Amazons are on horseback and some on foot. They are armed with defensive weapons such as helmets, shields, pelthae, and battle axes. Hyppolita, or Antiope their queen, is seen in the middle of the group, wounded, and carried away by Theseus. This interesting remnant of ancient art, is very remarkable for the variety of action, the movements of the figures, and their warlike character. It was found at *Papa Giulio*, a villa half a mile from the *Porta del Popolo*.

50. FINE COLUMN of a very rare red porphyry, standing on a base of white marble.

51-52. Pillar of red porphyry — Small column of *porta santa*.

MERCURY OF BELVEDERE

53. One of the most valuable and perfect pieces of antique greek sculplure. The great masters of painting *Domenichino* and *Poussin*, made this statue their particular and careful study, expecially the second, after he had affirmed, this statue to be the only one wich adequately exhibits the selfsame symmetrical proportions of the human body. It has long been supposed that it represented either the youthful Hercules, or Meleager, or Theseus, or Antinous, Hadrian's favourite, but Visconti with more probability, thought, or rather proved it to be really Mercury, the Messenger of the Gods, and the inventor of palestric games. He was led to this con-

clusion from the short hair, the calm and meditati-
ve features expressive of youth and beauty, the ro-
undness, and lightness of his delicate limbs, the drapery entwined and thrown over his left shoulder,
and the head slightly bending forward, an indica-
tion of his apotheosis, espressive of his conde-
scention in benignantly receiving the prayers and
supplications of mortals. The same opinion receives greater weight from a study of the other busts and statues which represented this God, and
especially of a bronze statue in the Borghese Gallery, as well, as from a consideration of the trunk
of the palm-tree, against which the present statue stands, since this God was the first who used
the leaves of that tree, as material for writing
upon. The only portions which are wanting are
the right arm, and the left hand. It is sculptured
in Parian marble, and was discovered at *S. Mar-
tino ai Monti*, on the Esquiline Hill, near the
Baths of Titus, in the year 1779.

Lining the walls of this Cabinet, there are:

54-55. *Opposite each one:* TWO BASRELIEFS
the one representing a combat between the Amazons and the Athenians, the other an *Isidis
pompa* or a sacred procession to the temple of
Isis made by some priests and priestesses. It exhibits various symbols and instruments for sacrificing as, the *hydria* the *sitella*, vases for water, the *capeduncula*, the *sistrum*, a representation
of the Nile overflowing, the lotus-flower, the wings of a hawk, and a serpent. From its style, we
may infer that this basrelief belongs to the third

stage of Egyptian sculpture, consequently it must be referred to the times of Adrian.

56. Priapus the god of the gardens. crowned with grapes. Found in the farm of the *Chiaruccia*, near Civitavecchia.

57. Hercules found in the V*ia Sacra* by the temple of Peace.

Outside the Cabinet:

58. ROMAN LADY lying on the cover of a sarcophagus. The very singular head-dress of this figure shows it to have belonged to the time of Titus. The basrelief, which adorns the front of the sarcophagus, bears the image of the dead engraved on it between two Cupids. Found beyond *Porta Maggiore*.

59. Cippus with inscription to *Blostus*.

60. Basrelief representing the image of the deceased with the four seasons assisting at the door of the tomb. Found on the Viminal, in the *Villa Montalto*

61. SEPULCHRAL URN, on which Thetys the sea-goddes, is represented with the Nereids, bearing to Achilles the armours, forged for him by Vulcan. A b. r. discovered at *Roma Vecchia*. Over it stands a very interesting fragment of a nymph seated on a sea monster. This is the work of a skilful greek chisel. It was found at *Palestrina*.

62. *Opposite this*: An ancient bath of red oriental granite standing on pattens of *africana breccia*. Found in the *Piazza Spada*.

63. Cinerary urn standing on a cippus which bears a latin inscription of *Livius Secundus* to *Caesonia Ploce* his wife.

*Close by the entrance of the Hall of the Ani-
mals there are on each side:*

In the wall above:

64-65. TWO COLOSSAL MOLOSSIAN DOGS ,
in excellent style. The one was found in the farm
della Chiaruccia near Civitavecchia; the other
in the *Pighini Palace.*

66. Pentagonal basrelief with a doubtful representation of Hercules. Found at Tivoli.

*The fresco in the wall is by Unterperger. It
represents the Tiber and the Glory.*

67. Vase of white marble.

Opposite the wall:

68 69. A basrelief — Sarcophagus with a representation of the battle of the Amazons.

70-71. Bath of red oriental granite. found in the
Piazza Spada — A cippus.

72. Sacrifice of Mithras.

73. SLEEPING NYMPH represented with the
Orgian serpent , a symbol of immortality, twined
round her left arm.

CABINET OF THE LAOCOON

74. This wonderful group sculptured in pentelic
marble embodies in the most excellent and exact
manner the famous description of Virgil in the
2nd. book of the Æneid. (*) Laocoon , priest of

(*) . . . . at primum parva duorum. .
Corpora natorum serpens amplexus uterque.
Implicat, etc.

Æn. II. 218.

Neptune, is here represented as fallen on the sacred altar, on which he was making a sacrifice,
in the act of striving to extricate himself and his
two young children from the innumerable coils of
the monstrous serpents sent against him by the
wrathful Pallas. It is a classic composition in which
the terror, the piety, and the desperate anguish of
a father, together with the noble dignity of a
priest, are faithfully portrayed. And in such a
manner is the nature of the action expressed, that
we seem to assist at the horrible scene· The breast convulsively contracted, the elevated eye-brows,
the contortion of the muscles, veins, ad ten-
dons of the arms and feet, admirably shows, how
great is the physical pain, by which he is agitated.
This original masterpiece of art, was found in the
fifteenth century in a vineyard at «*Le Selle Sale*»
amongst the ruins of the Baths of Titus, *on the
Esquiline*, in the same niche in which, as Pliny
says, it anciently stood and was admired, together
with other renowned works of art. It is the joint
work of three illustrious sculptors of Rhodes, vix:
Agesander and his two sons *Polydorus*, and *Athe-
nodorus*. When discovered, it excited such admiration among the geniuses of that age, that the
celebrated *Sadoleto* composed a noble poem on it
« *Ecce iterum terrae latebris* » etc. It was placed
here by the munificence of Pope Leo X. ·

* Its discoverer was a certain *Felix de Freddis*, as we may
read on his tombstone in the Church of Aracœli on the Capitol.
Its modern restoration are the right arm of the father in *terracotta* by *Bernini*, and those of both the sons in stucco, after those in
marble by *Cornacchini*. *Canova's* opinion was, that the arm of the

Issuing from the Cabinet, we behold:

75. Triumph of Bacchus, basrelief.

76. Baccanalian feast.

77-78. *To the niche :* Nymph Appiades with a found by the temple of Peace — Statue of Modesty.

Outside of the cabinet.

79. HERCULES and BACCUS *in altorilievo.* The hero is covered with the Nemæan lion's skin, bearing on his arm his son Telephus. The stag, and the head of the bull, allude to three of his labours. Bacchus stands by him, leaning upon a Faun, with a tiger at his feet.

80. Sarcophagus with basrelief found in the *Vigna Moroni* outside St. Sebastian.

81. LARGE BASRELIEF remarkable for the size of the figures, and its good style. It represents a sacred procession of lictors, and other persons going to a temple, in order to offer sacrifice, and thanksgiving to the Gods after a victory. It probably belongs to the time of Nero.

82. A large BATH in a single block, of a very fine white and black granite. The mark of division along its base, clearly shows, it had served also as a sarcophagus for two persons. Found in the *Mausoleum* of *Adrian.*

83. Medallion and pillar of red granite.

father should not be stretched out so far, but rather more inclined and resting on his head, because that unnatural tension could not produce the strength required to bend it. In the corner of the cabinet there is also another arm in marble, begun by a pupil of Michael Angelo in order to restore the group, but he left it unfinished. According to Pliny it was made of one block of marble but Michel Angelo with others says it results of three separate pieces.

84. ANCIENT MEDALLION in white marble representing on basrelief a dancing Mænade, and an altar between two pine-trees. It stands on a half-pillar of oriental red granite.

85. HYGEIA. A statue larger than life. The daughter of Æsculapius and goddess of health, is here represented with the usual symbol of the serpent, twined round her arm, and, drinking in the cup, which she offers to it by the other hand. The numerous statues of this goddess we meet with, were dedicated to her by wealthy men, on their restoration to health.

The present one is sculptured in parian marble. It is remarkable for the good stile of execution, and its singular beauty. The name of the divinity is connected with the mutual salutations used by Romans and Greeks, whose costume was to say in the morning, and in the evening, χαιρε, υγιαινι.

86. Sepulchral altar in the form of a house. On it there is a cinerary urn of *M. Apuleius Ermes.*

87. Altars with latin inscriptions. One states that it was erected to *Lucio Volusio Paridi*, attorney *of Lucius Volusius*, by *Claudia Elpide* his wife, *Volusia Amillu*, and *Volusia Paride* his daughters. It was found along with its opposite one in the *Amentola's vineyard*, on the *Appian Way.* They stand on two rare blocks of a beautiful kind of *dendrophore* or flowered alabaster , called « *a pecorelle* » from its white spots. Both were brought from *Porto Claudio*, near *Fiumicino* in 1825.

Between these two blocks of alabaster in the niche:

88. *Set in the wall*: LARGE SARCOFHAGUS supposed to have ornamented some imperial arch. It represents Rome personified in the act of bestowing the honour of the triumph, on a victorious emperor.

89. Bath in a single block of a red egyptian porphyry, removed from *Negroni's Villa* on the Viminal.

90. Ossuary with a latin inscription to *Q. Vitellio*, found on the Cælian Hill, in the *Villa Mattei*.

91. Sarcophagus found on the Flaminian Way. Small cinerary urns are placed on it.

Entering the:

CABINET

OF THE APOLLO OF BELVEDERE,

92. It is not in the power of words to describe the beauty of this celebrated statue, one of the most famous masterpieces of ancient greek sculpture, now extant. It is admirably executed, and represents the handsomest of the Gods in the attitude either of deafeating the giants, or taking revenge on the sons of Niobe, or on the serpent Python, to which the snake which is crawling up the trunk of the tree, may allude. The swelling nostrils, and the curving of the lower lip, nobly express his divine disdain, and contempt of the miserable object of his wrath, at the same time on the forehead and in the eyes, there reign that placid tranquillity, and dignity which characterize a God. He is leaning forward with maje-

sty. The position of the right arm, [1] indicates that
he has already shot an arrow, whilst he seems
also to grasp the bow by the left. This statue
may be truly called one of the first specimens of
male beauty, as the Venus Medicea of Cleomenes,
in the Gallery of Florence, may be considered the
most perfect model of female beauty. Every thing
connected with it, harmonises with the lightness
of the person, and all beauties one can imagine,
are adapted to this figure, so that in looking upon
it, the mind may indulge that pleasant enthusiasm,
which the contemplation of the beautiful invariably excites. The marble is of the best kind, viz
the pentelic, by some also admitted to be of the
quarries of *Carrara*. It was discovered towards
the end of tho fifteenth century among the ruins
of *Porto d'Anzio*, where anciently stood a splendid residence of the Roman Emperors, and of which
probably it was one of the finest ornaments. Discovered in the year 1506 under the reign of Julius II by whom it was purchased when a Car-
dinal, it has formed for three centuries, one of
the brightest gems of this Museum, where the

---

[1] Both the arms were restored by Giov. Angelo da Montorsoli
a pupil of Michael Angelo. With respect to its origin, it may be
a copy from a bronze of Paramythia, or the workmanship of Cala-
mides after one of Praxiteles, or by Agasias of Ephesus. Probably
it was brought from Greece by Nero; along with the Gladiator of
the Villa Borghese, and the five hundred bronze statues, which were
carried away from the temple dedicated to this God in Delphos.
The sole defect observed in this statue, is the unequal and unnatural lenght of the legs, but this inconveniency is easily compensa-
ted by the greater switness which thence accrues to the figure,
and which is more proper to a deity. The figure is 9. palms high.

illustrious Pontif, on his elevation to the Papal dignity, caused it to stand.

Set in the lateral walls, above :

93-94. TWO BASRELIEFS, one of wich represents an imperial lion-hunt. The equestrian figure, which stands in the centre in the act of darting an arrow, is supposed to be Alexander Severus, as this emperor was very fond of such sports. The other exhibits a bull, led to the sacrifice by two Bacchantes. From the excavations of *Terra di Lavoro.*

95-96. *In the niches :* Venus Victrix, found at Otricoli — Minerva.

97. The Nile, on a sarcophagus ornamented with a strigil, and Ganimede with the eagle.

98. *Set in the wall, above :* A Trapezophor or marble slab, which the ancients used to support their tables. It was discovered in the *Villa Negroni,* and exhibits two figures of Fauns or Satyrs who are pressing grapes on a crater, adorned with a garland, among two vine-leaves, thyrsi, and two winged dolphins, that stand at each extremity.

99. Sarcophagus found on the Cassian Way, exhibiting Bacchus, supported by Ampelus and a Bacchante.

100. BATH of green *basalte,* the *lapis basanitica* of Pliny, found in the *Thermae* of *Caracalla,* near *S. Cesareo.*

101-102. Doric column of a red porphyry with purple and green spots, very rare to be met with; discovered near *Ponterotto* on the left bank of the Tiber — Column of white marble ornamented with ivy-leaves.

HALL OF THE ANIMALS.

We enter this Hall from the opposite side of the *Portico Belvedere*, where two colossal dogs of Molossus are placed, and are cowering on each side, as if to guard the entrance.

This is the rarest and finest collection of sculptures of animals ever formed, a *menagerie* in marble, as it has been called, well arranged, and divided into two parts by a square vestibule, ornamented with four pillars and granite pilasters. For the richness of the marbles, delicacy of execution and variety, it has no rival. The animals are placed on brackets, consoles, and marble tables, supported by animals paws, with gripphins and lion's heads. The pavement in the middle of the vestibule, is inlaid with black and white mosaic pieces, representing an Eagle devouring a Hare, found in the *Marca di Ancona*, a Leopard, and a Wolf discovered at *Palestrina*.

Beginning to the right side, on the bracket close to the entrance :

103. Griffin in flowered alabaster, anciently considered as the guardian of sepulchres.

104. Eagle fighting with a monkey.

105-106. Toad, in *rosso antico* — Calf's head.

107. Two expressive groups of Stags attacked by two dogs, a very natural composition. The richly engraved pedestals on which these groups

are placed are by *Franzoni*, who restored the greater part of the animals collected in these Halls.

On the opposite side of one of the pedestals, there is an inscription in Latin verses, relating to the fable of Actæon, the subject of which it represents.

108. *On the upper bracket:* Bull attacked by a Bear.

109. *Above to the wall:* An Elephant fighting with a Leopard.

On the marble table:

110-111-112. A Goose — Ibis — Stork.

113. Mithraic Sacrifice.

114-115. Grey-hound — Hunting dog.

116-117. Two beautiful grey hounds playing together. A graceful group found with two others in this Hall, relating to the same subject (117 169), near *Civita Lavinia*, in a place named *Monte Canino*, probably so called from their discovery.

118. Ethiopian Ram so called by *Johnston*, but it must be the Aries of the Alps, *aries gutturatus* of *Fabbroni*. According to the same naturalist the head of the present animal, which now is in the Gallery of Florence, was of a black marble, here erroneously restored in white. The torso only is ancient.

119. A Dog in *paronazzetto* marble.

120. Basrelief representing a bacchanalian.

121-122-123. Ibis — Hawk, birds held in great veneration amongst the Egyptians —A Hen.

124. MITHRAIC SACRIFICE. This highly interesting group in Parian marble, exhibits to us

an allegorical representation of the influence of
the Sun over the Earth. Mithras the Persian
Sun-God, plunges a sword into the bull, which
represents the Earth. The dog and serpent, are
emblems of the various animals nourished by the
Earth under the genial rays of the Sun. The
scorpion gnawing the scrotum, is figure of Autumn bringing decay on the rich produce of the
Summer. The dog emblematic of the dog-star, and
the easy, flexible movements, and wavy form of
the serpent, a type of the Ocean, make up this
group very interesting and celebrated. The Vatican possesses many representations of this subject,
but this is by far the finest of all. It was found
at Ostia, where was a large subterraneum temple dedicated to the worhisp of that Persian
Deity.

*On each side of this group, set in the wall
above, are :*

113.A - 125.A. Two masterly executed mosaic
pieces recently found (1867) in Adrian's villa at
Tivoli. The one represents a lion assaulting and
tearing abull, and a Cow rushing down a hill, into
the sea. In the other, some goats are grazing among
ruins, and a figure holding a sceptre, probably Pale
or Ceres, the protectress deity of flocks. They were
placed here by the munificence of Pius IX.

125. Candelabrum with two Sphynxes.

126-127-128. Hawk — Goose — Ibis killing a
serpent.

128. *In the wall* : Pelicas, a basrelief.

On the marble table :

130. Europe, carried off by Jupiter, under the form of a bull. A small but very graceful group.

131. Bull, found at Ostia.

132. Stag running, sculptured in two precious kinds of oriental alabaster, the one, that of the body, is the *fiorito*, that of the horns is *colognino*. Brought from the Quirinal.

133. Lion, finely sculptured in very hard yellow *breccia*. The teeth and tongue are very natural, being made of different marbles. Found near the temple of Peace.

134. HERCULES dragging away the Nemæan lion; a group smaller than life.

135. Lion fish in *verde di Carrara*.

136. *Above on the bracket :* Wolf.

137. Hercules slaying Diomedes, a tyrant of Thrace, who fed his horses with human flesh. Found at *Ostia*.

A.137. HERCULES bringing away the tripod of Delphos.

138. CENTAUR, represented with a Cupid on his back, and holding in his left hand a hare, a modern addition. It is a good copy of the Centaurs by *Papias* and *Aristeas*, greek sculptors. It stands on a pedestal composed of various kinds of marble. Found in the excavations of the Lateran.

139. COMMODUS on horseback in the act of throwing a javelin against a wild animal. *Bernini* took this small equestrian statue, as a model for his colossal one of Costantine the Great, which stands under the right Porch of St. Peter's. Found in the villa *Mattei*.

Passing the arch leading to the Gallery of the Statues :

140. *Above*: Eagle found at *Monte Citorio*.

141-142-143. Hercules found at *Ostia* — Sphynx of a *giallo antico* — Tiger.

144-145-146. A Water-hen — Tiger in egyptian granite — Cow.

Above on the tables :

147-148. A Rat found in the so called *Sepolcro di Nerone* on the Cassian Way — Hawk.

Down before the window:

149-150. Lion in yellow breach — Hare hung to the trunk of a tree.

151. Lamb immolated on an altar, a *caeremonia aruspicina*, found in the *villa Mattei*.

152. Duck in a shell of plaster.

153. SHEPHERD SLEEPING with goats grazing around him, probably Endymion, the beautiful lover of Diana. It is a group worthy of particular notice for the gracefulness of the composition, and its good state of preservation.

A.153. Hare eating grapes recently discovered in the excavations of the *Emporium* of marbles commonly called the *"Marmorata"* near the Gate of St. Paul.

154. Panther sculptured in flowered alabaster marked with black and yellow spots, to imitate the natural colour of that animal.

155. Tiger of egyptian granite.

156. A large Lion in *bigio marble*, represented with a calf's head beneath its paws. Found at the Lateran.

Set in the lateral wall of the window :

157. Rural scene, a basrelief. This very interesting subject illustrated by Visconti, represents the pagan costume of the lustration, or purification of a cow by water. The scene takes place beside a fountain, near a rustic temple. An old tree stretches its thick branches over the cool waters; a peasant bears in one hand a cup full of water, in the other, an olive branch and his offering of two geese, hanging from his pastoral staff. It was discovered at *Tivoli.*

158. *Opposite this:* Cupid in a chariot drawn by two wild boars. The *spina* round which they run, is here shown by an *ara* adorned with arabesques.

159-160. Duck catching a Frog — Raven with a Hedge-hog.

161-162-163. A Bull — Camel — Tiger.

164. Group of a Stag assaulted by Dogs.

165-166-167. Pheasant — A Horse upon an urn with inscription to *Quinto Cornelio Nubiano* — Gray-partridge.

168. A Fish sculptured in *verde serpentino.*

169. A Grey-hound.

170-171. Lion in a grey-marble — Cow suckling a Calf.

172. *Down:* Head of an ass, perhaps the ass of Silenus.

In the vestibule before the pilasters :

174-175. *On the table:* Goat seized by a Tiger— Equestrian figure.

Before the arch of entrance to the Hall of the Muses:

176. Oval vase standing on a pillar of beautiful flowered alabaster.

Crossing the vestibule on entering the second division of the Hall. On either side, before the pilasters :

177. Head of a Goat, put on a column of white marble, found at Tivoli.

In the vestibule, placed on a bracket:

178-179. Horse running, sculptured in touch stone — Bacchus riding on a goat.

Crossing the vestibule:

180. Goat supposed to be the Amaltæa which suckled Jupiter, from the small fragment of a child's hand, fastened to its mane. Found on the *Caelian Hill.*

Into the middle of the Hall : A fine large table of a rare *verde antico morato* marble, in a single block, found near *Civitavecchia*, on the sea shore.

181-182-183-184. A Cow—Mule's head — Hare— Winged Sphynx.

185-186. Hare eating grapes — A Pig.

On the marble table:

187-188-189. A Wolf — Goat — Cat.

190-191. Tiger found in Adrian's villa at Tivoli— A wild Cat devouring a Fowl.

192. Dolphin attacked by a sea griffin, sculptured in rare oriental alabaster.

193. A Lamb torn in pieces by a Tiger.

194. *On a marble table :* A SOW surrounded by twelve of her young, perhaps allusive to that celebrated white one, which appeared to Æneas,

in his first landing to Hesperia in *Latium,* where his son Ascanius aftervards founded *Alba Longa.*

195. *Before the iron-grating:* A Horse attacked by a Lion. A very expressive group.

The large mosaics inlaid in the middle of these two Halls, were called by the ancients the *" Analecta mensae "* and served as pavements of the dining-rooms. They are divided into twelve compartments, each representing in various colours, chickens, fishes, vegetables. *Analecti* also the Greeks called the slaves, whose office was to clean the halls, after the dinners. The present ones were discovered in the escavations of *Roma Vecchia,* four miles and a half beyond the *Porta Maggiore.*

On the tables above :

196-197-198. A Sphynx — Dove — Head of an Ox.

199-200-201. A Cock — Turtle — Crocodile.

202. Camel's head. It served as a fountain for water.

In the middle of the Hall:

203-204. Two small columns with corinthian capitals.

205-206-207. Water-fowl — A Boar — A Sea-horse.

208. *In the niche :* HERCULES killing Geryon, and taking from him, his carnivorous oxen.

209. A COW sculptured in brown marble. The head is modern. It is perhaps, as Visconti supposes, a fine imitation of that celebrated one in bronze by Myron. Found near the lake of *Nemi.*

210-211. Statue of Diana chasing — A Horse-Tiger.

212. Lion, found on the Caelian Hill.

213. *In the niche :* HERCULES, bringing the three-headed dog Cerberus in chains, from the infernal regions. Found at Ostia.

Set in the wall above :

214. Eagle eating a Hare, with a serpent twined to an oak.

215. Head of a Wild-roe in *rosso antico* found at *le Pantanelle near Tivoli.*

216-217-218. A Bear — Head of a Ram — Fragment of a basrelief.

219-220. A Pea-hen, found at Tivoli— Ampelus sporting with a Lion.

221-222-223. A Pelican — An Ape— A Peacock, found at Tivoli.

Set in the wall above :

224. Basrelief with an Elephant.

225-226-227. A Goat's head — Eagle found in the *Villa Mattei* — Head believed to represent a Rhinoceros.

228. TRITON, or Marine Centaur carrying off a Nereid in his arms. A beautiful group. The lower limbs of the Nereid are half clothed in a long flowing tunic. The outstretched and delicate arms, admirably express her feelings of alarm, and distress. The Triton is holding to mouth a large sea-shell, an allegorical representation of the noise of the winds. Two little Cupids, both seated on the tail of the monster, look out for help for the ravished Nymph, but they appear to look in vain. This rare and remarkable group gives us a good idea of the original one made by *Scopas.* It served perhaps to ornament some fountain. It stands

on the sepulchral cover of a sarcophagus, around
the oval lid of which, is represented in basrelief
the celebration of the festivities of Bacchus. Amongst the figures which adorn it, those of Hercules
overcome by wine, and the little Genius playing
with his lion, are very remarkable. Il was discovered outside the Latin Gate, in the *Effetti's vineyard.*

229. Cray-fish larger than life, sculptured in
rare green porphyry.

230-231. A Lynx — The Wolf giving suck to
Romulus and Remus.

232. MINOTAUR, rare fragment of this monster, which according to the greek myth, was represented as a human figure with the head of a
bull. Probably the fragment represents here the
monster, in the act of fighting with Theseus, by
whom it was aftervards killed. The paintings of
Herculaneum tend also to confirm our description.

233. Priest sacrificing a bull. Instead of the bull,
the figure should represent a cow, which a priest
is milking to prepare a libation. The first use of
these libations, according to Pliny, was introduced
by *Romulus and Remus*, and was invariably observed, even when the city was at the height of
its power. It probably stood to ornament some sepulchre, the milk libation being acceptable as an
offering to the *manes* of the dead.

On the marble bracket:

234. A group of goats. They stand on a vase
richly sculptured, and elegantly adorned with figures of birds and fishes. It was discovered at
Adrian's villa.

235-236-237-238. A Hedge-hog — Satyr with a Cow — Head of a Horse — Goat suckling a Kid.

239. Goat bitten by a serpent.

On the opposite side:

246-241-242-243. Group of Storks, a Serpent, and Kid — A Hare — Head of a Cow — Group of a Dog attacked by a mastiff.

In the middle of the Hall, at each side of the mosaic inlaid on the pavement:

244-245. A large table of a rare *verde antico morato*, cut with the opposite corresponding one.

246-247. Beautiful Tripods of *pavonazzetto* marble, supported by three double Hermes of Bacchus, like Atlantes — The other is in *verde Ponserera*.

GALLERY OF THE STATUES.

The present Gallery once served as a sum-
merhouse to Innocent VIII. In the fifteenth century it was nobly ornamented with beautiful paintings by *Manteyna, Pinturicchio, Giulio Romano*
and their pupils. Clement XIV *(Ganganelli)* greatly
enlarged it, and afterwards Pius VI added some rich
and elegant decoration by *Wunterperger.*

The pavement is inlaid with marble of rich
and various colours. Lastly to the munificence of
Pope Pius IX, is due the elegant decoration of
the lateral walls in the style of *Herculaneum,* as
also its most splendid ornament, vix the magnificent Bath of the rarest quality of oriental alabaster, which stands in the middle of the Hall.

On the right hand :

248. CLODIUS ALBINUS, the colleague of Septimius Severus, with a countenance pensive and
melancholy. Found at *Castro muoro,* near *Cirita-
vecchia.* It stands on a pedestal of travertine
which bears an inscription, stating that the body
of C. Cæsar, son of Germanicus and great son of
Augustus was burnt within. Found with some
others in the Mausoleum of Augustus.

249. A modern basrelief sculptured by *Michael
Angelo Buonarroti* whose image may be seen
among the bearded figures. It represents *Cosi-
mo II* Duke of Tuscany, in the act of expelling

from *Pisa* the allegorical figures of the Vices, and welcoming the Virtues, Sciences, and Arts.

250. CUPID, a beautiful fragment in Parian marble, supposed to be the original work of Praxiteles. In describing its superior workmanship, its serious-melancholy beauty, we cannot easily do it justice. It has much suffered from time, and neglect. Brought from Greece by Caligula, it was lost during the conflagration of the city. Pliny speaks of it as it was for a long time admired in the *Portico* of *Octaria*, with many other precious works of art. It was found two miles beyond the *Porta Maggiore*, in a place called *Centocelle*, perhaps the site where the palace of Elagabalus stood. Some suppose, it represents the Genius of Death. But it is generally known by the name of the *Genius of the Vatican*. It was evidently a Cupid, as the holes for the wings are still visible on the shoulders. Besides, it bears that superior and expressive look, a character more suitable to the son of Venus, than to the son of Night.

251. Athlete in repose. A statue on its pedestal there is a head of a Satyr sculptured in *alto rilievo*.

252. The Rape of Proserpina, a basrelief.

253. TRITON. A half figure of life-size, very remarkable for its peculiar style of sculpture, and the small number of such representations to be met with. Discovered at *St. Angelo in Capoccia*, near *Tivoli*.

254. Statue of a Bacchante.

255. PARIS. A sitting statue larger than life representing the celebrated son of Priam, dressed

in the Persian costume, allusive to the triumph
of the Greeks over the Persians. It wears the
tunica succincta, the *chlamis*, the Phrygian cap,
the sandals, and holds in the right hand the apple
of Discord. This statue formerly was in the *Altemps
Palace*. It stands on an altar dedicated to Hercules under Trajan, by more than sixty workmen
of the imperial mint. Their names may be seen
sculptured on its right side.

256. Hercules in his youth.

257. Diana drawn in the chariot by a Victory.

*The arms of Julius II, held by Angels, by
Julio Romano. A fresco in the wall.*

258. Bacchus, torso of a sublime character found
in the gardens of the *Mendicanti*.

259. MINERVA PACIFERA. A statue larger
than life. The bronze-helmet, and the olive branch
she holds in her hands allude to her character,
as Peace bearer, *Pacifera*. The only portions of
modern restoration, are the head, and right arm.

260. Suplicants adressing some deities supposed
to be Æsculapius, Hygeia, and the Dioscuri, a
basrelief.

261. PENELOPE. The wife of the wise Ulysses
is represented seated and resting her head upon
her right hand, in a state of deep affliction, meditating on the long absence of her beloved husband. The very severe style of greek art, in which
this statue is sculptured, shows it to be anterior
to the time of Phidias. Besides this statue, there
is also in the *Chiaramonti Museum* a basrelief
on the same subject, and some others in connection with the history of Ulysses, in the *Arche-*

rian Museum of the Roman College, and also in the *Barberini Library.*

262. CALIGULA C. CÆSAR. The third emperor and tyrant of Rome. He stands in an heroic attitude, entirely naked with the *parazonium* and *chlamys*, tied up to the left arm. The images of this emperor are rare to be met with, having all been destroyed after his death by order of the Senate. This is supposed to be the only one, now in existence. It bears a close resemblance to the ancient imperial coins. It was found in the Augusteum of *Olricoll.* On the cippus below, is engraved in low relief the figure of an *aurifex bractearius*, a gold beater.

263. Diana in a *quadriga*, a basrelief.

264. APOLLO SAUROKTONOS, viz lizard-slayer. The handsome God is represented when in the flower of his youth exiled by Jupiter to the island of Delos, he is in the act of shooting an arrow, and piercing a lizard creeping on the bark of the tree, on which the God rests with his left arm. The life like appearance of this statue, the gentle movements, the delicacy and finish of its composition, make it a very good copy of the original *bronze statue* of Praxiteles, so celebrated for its excellence and beauty, throughout all Greece. This is better preserved than that, which stands in the *Borghese* Gallery. It was discovered in the *Villa Spada* on the Palatine Hill, in the excavations made there by *Gavin Hamilton* in 1727.

265. AMAZON. A well preserved statue sculptured in a fine quality of *grechetto* marble. It is represented like that one of the *Braccio Nuovo.*

and of the Museum of the Capitol, clothed in a military dress. At her feet lie the helmet, the *bipennis*, a battle axe, and the *pelta*, a sort of buckler. The strap on the left foot, served to fasten the single spur, which was used by the Amazons when riding. This is the work of a skilful Greek chisel, undoubtedly a copy of the highly renowned work by *Policletes*, or from one of the fifty bronze-statues which adorned the temple of Diana at Ephesus. Both the arms and right leg are of modern addition. It was brought here from the *Mattei Villa*. The inscription on the left side of the plinth states this statue was anciently removed from the «*Schola Medicorum*» to another place, where it afterwards remained.

266. Centaur with a winged Victory.

267. DRUNKEN FAUN. A reclining statue which formerly served as an ornament to some fountain. Found on the Celium.

268. Juno. A statue found in the Baths of Otricoli. On the pedestal Diana is represented chasing, in *alto riliero*.

269. LAODAMIA and PROTESILAUS. A very interesting basrelief in which Protesilaus, one of the Greek heroes, the first who was killed by Æneas and Hector at the siege of Troy, is represented by the artist as coming back from Elysium for three hours, granted him by the Gods. He is in the act of talking to his faithful wife Laodamia under a tree, round which a serpent, the symbol of immortality, is twined. It belongs to the finest style of the happiest age of Greece.

270. URANIA seated on a rock with the *stylus*, and globe in her hands. The singular ornament of this valuable statue, smaller than life, are the feathers on the head, allusive perhaps to the victory of the Muses, over the Syrens.

On either side of the arch which divides the present Gallery from the Hall of the Busts, there are two statues, representing:

271-390. POSIDIPPUS AND MENANDER two masters of Greek Comedy. Both are sitting in their *hemicicles*, or chairs, in negligent postures, as if meditating, or resting themselves. They are carefully dressed. Menander, as *Visconti* supposes, is attired in the Macedonian costume with the tunic and sandals. Posidippus, as an Athenian, with the *pallium quadratum*, a finger ring, and half leg-buskins. Menander was born at Athens *B. C.*342. On his death Posidippus repaired thither, and became a most distinguished comedian. The names given to these statues are authentical, since we find them engraved on the plynths. The penthelic marble in which these statues are executed, the form of the chairs, the marks of *meniscos*, a sort of glory-disk, to save them from the injuries of time, and the bronze traces of plates on the legs, to protect them from the crushing of the people, all prove they were formerly placed to the entrance of the theatre at Athens. These statues the finest extant relating to comedy, are remarkable for their good preservation, and excellent style of sculpture. They were both found in a round Hall of the Thermae of Olympia, on the *Viminal Hill.*

Passing to the:

HALL OF BUSTS

1.ᵗ *Division* :

A small section of the Museum, but very interesting both in a historical and mythological point of view.

Beginning on the right of the entrance on the opposite end of the upper marble-shelf:
272. JULIUS CÆSAR. A draped bust.
Lower down on the second shelf:
273. AUGUSTUS. A head very rare, on account of the crown which encircles it, being a distinctive quality of his character as a « *Frater Arralis* » The ears of corn may also allude to the plenty granted to the Roman people by his conquest of Egypt, or more likely to the large amount of corn, as well as of money, distributed to the people in times of scarcety. Found on the *Celian Hill* in the *Villa Mattei.*

274. AUGUSTUS. Another valuable bust representing the emperor, at a more advanced period of his age. The centre of the laurel-crown which encircles the head, is decorated with a large orbicular gem, which bears the image of Julius Cæsar. This undoubtedly refers to his dignity of Highpriest of the Divus Julius, his adoptive father.

276. Nero , head larger than life. The wicked emperor is represented wearing a crown of laurel, under the appearance of Apollo Cytharædus.

277. Otho , the successor of Galba. The drapery and armour are of a beautiful oriental *colognino* alabaster.

8

278. Titus, a life-size head.

279. Nerva Cocceius, of head life size.

230-231. Trajan, a bust. — Adrian. A bust larger than life, found at Tivoli.

282. Antoninus, Pius. A bust vith cuirass and helmet.

283. Lucius Verus, a valuable draped bust, found at *Roma Vecchia*.

Opposite, before this first section of busts : A fluted spiral column , of the rarest *nero antico Affricano*. Found on the *Aventine*. It is surmounted by a head of Satyr, larger than life in *rosso antico*, discovered in the neighbourhood of *Genazzano*.

284-285. M. Aurelius, found at *Adrian's Villa*. Commodus, a head.

286-287. Didius Julianus — Pescennius Nero.

288. Clodius Albinus. A bust with the name of the emperor engraved on the base.

289. Septimius Severus. A bust found at *Otricoli*.

290. CARACALLA. A bust, one of the best known, as it bears a close resemblance to the coins of this emperor. It deserves particular attention on account of the attitude, in which the emperor has been represented, vix of bending the head towards the left shoulder, indicating the foolish vanity of this Emperor, in striving to imitate Alexander the Great. It was discovered near the temple of Peace.

201. Alexander Severus. A bust from the excavations of *Ostia* of the year 1868.

292. Vespasian. A bust with the chlamys of

verde antico, and the armours of porta santa marble.

2nd. Division.

On the upper shelf of marble :

294. Female bust bearing great resemblance to one of the two figures of Cato and Portia which stand in the first division.

206. An unknown female bust, with a turtle on the head as a cap.

298. Jupiter Serapis. A colossal bust in black basalt. Found on the *Celio.*

299. Life-size head of Ptolemy king of Mauritania.

300. Manlia Scantilla, wife of Didius Julianus, a draped portrait-bust.

301. Julia Mammea. A well preserved bust, found at Otricoli.

302. Bust unknown.

On the lower range :

303. Apollo. A head which still retains traces of the ancient encausto varnish. It came from *Roma Vecchia.*

304. Otho. A bust with the *lorica* and *chlamys* in rose oriental alabaster.

307. Saturnus. A colossal veiled head.

· 308. Isis. A well draped bust larger than life. The goddess is crowned with a diadem, and the lotus-flower which stands on a crescent moon. Found at *Roma Vecchia.*

309-310. Bust unknown — LYSIMACHUS, king of Thrace. A life size head.

311. MENELAUS. A beautiful helmeted head, found at *Tivoli* in Adrian's villa. It is supposed to have belonged to a group of Menelaus supporting the corpse of Patroclus, a subject similar to the celebrated fragment of the group commonly known as the "*Pasquino*" which stands in front of the *Braschi Palace* near the *Piazza Navona*. The helmet of the present one is elegantly adorned with basrelief, allusive to the combat between Hercules and the Centaurs.

Passing from this to the third division:

Above, on the upper range there are some very singular heads and busts.

313-314. A Female-Singer — A mask entirely hollow, with teeth, ears, curled hair, and beard.

315-316. A Smiling Faun — A head of a Satyr with a very ludicrous countenance.

317-318. Augustus — Faun.

On the lower bracket:

319. Isis. A bust veiled and crowned with serpents.

320. Silenus with the pardalys.

321-322. Septimius Severus and Julia Pia his wife.

323. Fauness.

324-325. Marcus Aurelius.

In the central niche of the Hall:

326. JUPITER. A colossal sitting statue of the Father of the Gods represented in a majestic countenance, holding the thunderbolts and the sceptre with the eagle at his feet. This valuable statue belongs to the oldest and best style of greek sculpture. It was one of the finest monuments placed

in this Hall, which gave rise to this renowned collection.

Turning to the left, on the upper shelf :

327-329. Flamen with the tiara — A captive King. Found in the environs of the arch of Costantine, which it probably served to adorn.

330. Drusus, the brother of Tiberius.

331-332. *Below:* Head and Bust unknown — Silvanus.

333. CRISPINA, the wife of Commodus.

334-336. Domitia — MARCIA OTTACILLA, wife of Philipp the Elder.

337. ETRUSCILLA, the wife of Decius,

In front of the statue of Jupiter :

339. A Celestial Sphere or globe, adorned with the principal planets, and the great circle or zone, containing the twelve signs of the Zodiac. It is a very remarkable monument.

On each side of this, there are :

Two Oval Vases, the one is of *breccia affricana* with the pedestal of *porta santa* marble. The other is of alabaster of *Civilavecchia*, and stands on a pillar of white alabaster called *ghiacciuolo.*

Above on the table :

340-341. Busts unknown.

On reentering the right side of the 2nd Division.

342. JULIUS CÆSAR. A draped bust of oriental cotognino alabaster.

343. *Below:* Bust unknown.

344. Hercules adorned with the *corona tortilis.*

345. ANNIUS VERUS C.ÆSAR. A bust of life-size of the son of Marcus Aurelius, sculptured in the kind of marble called by the ancients *corallico*, which is the smallest and most minute grain known in statuary.

Within the arch :

346-347. Jupiter Ammon in *alto rilievo* — Mercury in bas relief.

In the niche :

350. LIVIA DRUSILLA, fourth wife of Augustus, represented under the allegorical figure of Piety, with the arms extended in the act of praying. *Below* there is a very interesting b. r. in wich the figures of the three Fates, viz, Clotho, Lachaesis , Atropos, and those of Prometheus, Mercury and Psyche, allegorically represent the three principal vicissitudes of human life, viz, *Birth, Life, and Death.*

On the upper shelf :

352 Head unknown.

353. Julia the daughter of Titus. A draped bust in *porta santa* marble.

To the corner:

354. Sabina, the wife of Adrian, a bust bearing a diadem on the head. Found at Tivoli.

A.354-355. Busts unknown.

356. Aristophanes. A well preserved portrait-bust of the dramatic poet of Athens, the author of fifty four comedies, of which only eleven are now extant. Found at Tivoli.

On the lower range to the right :

357-358. Antinöus , a bust — Orator, bust.

359-360. Sabina — Alexander Severus.

Beyond the arch, at the angle, on the upper range:

362-363. Hercules. — Diana, found at *Roma Vecchia.*

366-367-368. SCIPIO AFRICANUS, a very fine bust — SALONINUS, son of Gallienus, bust of life size. — Commodus.

On the lower range :

369-370. Julia Mammea, a portrait bust — Head unknown.

471 Julia the daughter of Titus.

In the centre of the second division: Fountain of white marble, supported by sea-horses.

Reentering the first division, on the lower marble-shelf:

On the marble table:

272-273-274. Bust unknown.

375. Isis. A head admirable both for the finish of workmanship and the excellent style of pre-servation. The hair is dressed in the form of a lotus-flower which rises from the top of the head.

376. MINERVA. A colossal bust bearing the helmet with the breast adorned with the ægis. In this valuable piece of art, delicacy of beauty is combined with sublimity of expression, and admirable execution. It was found in Adrian's Mausoleum.

377. Head unknown.

378. *On the rhound:* Colossal leg worthy to be admired for its excellent style, found near the *Partone.*

379. Head resembling Galba.

Between the two windows on the upper shelf:

380. Apollo citharædus , found near the temple of Peace.

381. *Below:* Head unknown.

382-84. Fragments of human anatomy. These two fragments of representation of human anatomy in marble , are the only ones of the kind known, the one exhibits the chest of a skeleton, and the other the organs of respiration.

On the shelf above:

383. PHILIPPUS THE YOUNGER. A bust sculptured in red porphyry, very valuable as a work of art, though it pertains to the period of decay. It stood in the *Barberini* palace.

On the left side of the window:

385-386-387. Heads unknown.

388. A valuable GROUP in one block of marble representing sepulchral portrait busts of a married couple, erroneously styled Cato and Porcia. Discovered on the Celian Hill.

In front of the windows:

389. A column in the form of a candelabra. Round it are sculptured in high relief female dancers or Nymphs. On the top of tho column, is a trophy or cuirass, of the rarest kind of alabaster, called of *Orte* , a small town near *Civita Castellana* , well known for its quarries now exhausted. *

On the pavement there are some valuable remains of the group of Patroclus, consisting of le-

---

* This column is of the same quality of marble as the two small pillars in the Confession of St. Peter's as, also a vase, which stands in the Gallery of the Candelabras in this Museum.

*gs and shoulders, on one side of which may be,
recognised the wound inflicted by Euphorbus. The
feet and legs deserve great admiration for the
easy of death.*

*Following the turn of the Gallery of Statues,
to the right side:*

390. *See Nber. 277.*

391. NERO, a sitting figure. The Emperor is represented in his favourite costume, as an Apollo
Cytharædus, crowned with laurel, and playing on
the lyre, as he is represented on the ancient imperial coins. With the exception of the bronze
statue in the Roman Museum, this is the most
valuable extant for the close resemblance it bears
to the rare images of this emperor. It is one of
the few that escaped from the destruction ordered by the Senate, and by the enraged people. It
was discovered in the Villa *Montalto.*

392. SEPTIMIUS SEVERUS.

393. DIDO. The unhappy queen of Carthage is
represented lying on the funeral pire, meditating
suicide, after the departure of her beloved Æneas.
According to the beautiful description of her misfortunes, given us by Virgil, only the left foot of
this statue bears a sandal, like the other statue
in the *Barberini Gallery.*

394. NEPTUNE, represented with his particu-
rar emblems, the dolphin and trident.

395. Apollo Cytharædos of an early etruscan
style.

396. WOUNDED ADONIS. The affrighted countenance of the favourite of Venus, and the pain
from his wound, as well as the apprehension of

approaching death , are admirably expressed , although not in accordance with the description given by Theocritus. This statue, sometimes called the *Barberini Narcissus* , is both admirable for its excellent workmanship, as well for good preservation.

397. BACCHUS. A life-size statue, not well preserved but remarkable for its good style of art. The God is as resting on one of the summits of Mount Parnassus. It was discovered at *Tivoli* in the Villa of Cassius together with the statues of the *Muses*, *the Apollo Cytharaedus*, *Pallas*, *and Somnus*.

398. OPILIUS MACRINUS, the successor of Caracalla. A rare statue , but not well sculptured. Found in the *Borioni's vineyard*.

399. ÆSCULAPIUS and HYGEIA. A beautiful group the only one known *in alto rilievo* of these deities. The figures are cut in a single piece of marble. Found in the Forum of Præneste.

400. Statue of Euterpe. On the pedestal there is a female head in *alto rilievo*.

401. ÆMON AND ANTIGONES. Beautiful fragment of a group representing the Theban Hero, in the act of killing himself over the corpse of his beloved Antigones, put to death by her cruel father Creon. *Canova's* opinion is, that this group formerly formed part of the celebrated group of the children of Niobe which stands in the Gallery of Florence. Some other authorities in art recognize in it the mournful tale of Procris , killed in mistake by her husband Cephalus, here represented as falling at his feet , on a rock. The

present statue was discovered in the neighbourhood of the *Porta S. Paolo.*

402. SENECA. The Roman philosopher. A statue nearly life-size, wearing the toga. Brought
from *Palo.*

403. *Set in the wall above:* LABERIA FELICLA,
high-priestess of Cybele, the mother of the Gods.
The temple and the college of Virgins attacked
to her worship in the town of Placia in the Pro-
pontis near Cyzicum was very celebrated. Her
priestess in here represented as standing in a
niche dressed is all the ensigns of her dignity.

404. Statue of Faenia, lying on a funeral couch,
bearing a crown of flowers.

405. DANAID. A half-dressed life-size figure representing one of the fifty unhappy daughters of
Danaus, king of Argos, who in punishement for
the murder of their husdands, except Hypermn-
estra, were all doomed to draw water from Lethe
and fill sieves, as it is expressed in this statue.
The pain caused, by long and bitter weeping and
useless labour, is naturally represented in the peculiar inclination of the head, and half closed eye-
lids. Both the arms and the vase improperly restored as a *lebelhes* and not as a sieve, are its modern additions. It was discovered in the Forum
of Præneste, and is perhaps a copy taken from
the fity celebrated bronze statues representing Da-
naids, which adorned the portico of the temple of
Apollo Palatinus in Rome.

406. FAUN. A beautiful repetition of the celebrated work by Praxiteles. Found at *Falerona* in
the *Marca d'Ancona.*

407. PERSEUS, represented with the wings on his head, the *harpe* or curved sword, and the talares *talaria* on the feet, lent him by Mercury, hasten the death of Medusa. The head does not agree with the other portions of the well executed figure. Discovered at *Civitavecchia*.

Continuing the round of the Gallery, we met with:

408. POPPEA, represented as Hygeia. Perhaps this statue is one of those erected to the memory of this unfortunate Princess by her wicked husband. Discovered on the *Cassian way* near the sepulchre of Nero, improperly so called. It stands on a cippus bearing an inscription which states, that the body of the son of Germanicus Cæsar was burnt within it. Found with the other adjoining cippi, near the Mausoleum of Augustus.

409. Fauu, a statue holding the *rhyton*.

410. FLORA. The lovely bride of Zephirus, and goddess of the gardens, is represented in this beautiful statue crowned with garlands, and holding a bunch of flowers. The cippus on which it stands, informs us that the ashes of Livilla the daugther of Germanicus, were kept in the large vase of oriental alabaster, which stands in front of the large window of this Gallery. It was found in the Mausoleum of Augustus.

411. Cinerary urn supported by a cippus with an inscription to *Publio Vitellio*, erected to him by *Vitellia Cleopatra* his wife.

412-413. BARBERINI CANDELABRAS, with basreliefs on the bases, representing Jupiter, Juno,

Mercury, Mars, Venus, Minerva. Found in Adrian's
Villa.

414. ARIADNE. A reclining statue larger than
life, in parian marble. For more than three centuries, this beautiful monument has been the subject of misapprehension and disnute among the
best critics of works of ancient art. It was conje-
ctured by some that this figure represented Cleopatra of Egypt from the bracelet or armlet in the
form of a serpent encircling the left arm, and
also from bearing a close resemblance to the attitude, in which according to Galenus, that unhappy
queen was found dead. *Winckelmann* took it for
a Naiade who presiding over a fountain had been
lulled asleep by the murmur of the waters. This
erroneous opinion was refused by Visconti, who
with his usual skill, proved this statue to be
Ariadne the daughter of Minos, sleeping on a rock
on the sea shore of Naxus when abandoned by
her unfaithful lover. This decision was confirmed
by the excavation of a fresco at *Herculaneum*,
and also by the small basrelief let into the wall
on the left side of this monument, both alluding
to the same subject. *(See. N.ʳ 416.)* The natural
countenance of this figure, greatly adds to its beauty
and simplicity. A large veil, parted from the rock
on which she is reclining, falls in rich folds and
is skilfully spread over the lower limbs of the
figure. The light *tunica* leaves the bosom half-
uncovered ; one of the arms supplies the place of
a pillow, the other rests negligently over her
head. Although the closed eyes seem to indicate
that she has sunk in a deep sleep, yet her beau-

tiful features express in the highest degree the
sorrow and hopeless despondency into which the
departure of her lover has thrown her. This wonderful statue purchased by Julius II, is one of the
finest that stood in the Gardens of the Pope, where
the poets and artist of that age used to assemble.
Castiglione has written a beautiful latin Poem on
its discovery, which with those of *Favoriti* and
Baldi were engraved in marble and placed along
side of the statue beyond the two Candelabra. It
was discovered by *Volpato* at *Lunghezza,* a farm
of the *Strozzi* near *Palestrina.* The large sarcophagus on which it stands exhibits a lively representation of the war of the giants against the
Gods, sculptured in basrelief.

416. *Set into the lateral wall* : An elegant basrelief expressly placed near the statue of Ariadne,
by Gregory XVI, to show their mutual connection. Indeed the countenance of the principal figure which stands in the middle, strongly resembles that of Ariadne, as the helmeted of Theseus
ascending the ship, seems to indicate her abando-
nment. The Faun who looks astonished from behind a grotto at the sleeping Ariadne, alludes to
her recovery effected by Bacchus , on his return
from the Indies. His figure , ; s well that of one
of his female followers are seen standing in both
the lateral spiral columns ,.by which this valuable basreliefs is divided. The wild goat with the
figure standing on the clouds (perhaps of Venus)
are referring to the island of Naxus , on which
Ariadne was deserted. A frame of leaves adorns
the upper and lower partitions with the group of

little Cupids darting a panther. The figure of Bacchus was restored by *Leonardi* in the sixteenth century. It was found at Adrian's Villa.

417. MERCURY. Among all the various accoutrements of the God, the lyre and the tortoise shell, are emblems very rare to be met with. The name of *Ingenui* records the sculptor who made it. The sepulchral inscription on the cippus, alludes to the burial place of the corpse of Tiberius Cæsar, son of Caius Germanicus.

418. Bacchanalian, a basrelief found in the *Villa Maltei*.

419. TORSO supposed to be of a Bacchus, in an exquisite style of sculpture. The fragment of basrelief on the socle, represents the celebration of the *Ludi Circenses*.

420. LUCIUS VERUS. A statue larger than life, valuable for its excellent style of sculpture, and the striking resemblance it bears to the portraits of this voluptuous colleague and son in law of M. Aurelius, the emperor philosopher. He stands in a military dress adorned with a richly embossed cuirass and the *palulamentum* thrown over his shoulders. The title of Parthicus which he undeservedly assumed, refers to the victories gained over the Parthians by his gallant legate Avidius Cassius, whilst he expended his time at Antiochia in lascivious festivals, in one of which he spent, it is said, the enormous sum of more than 1,200,000 francs. The inscription of the cippus tells us, that Tiberius Cæsar son to Drusus, was burnt within.

128

Before the large window adjoining the Cabinet of the Masks:

421. PUTEALE, or cylindrical mouth of a well called by the ancients, *Putea'ia sigillata,* from the basreliefs with which they were adorned. Interesting scenes from a bacchanalian feast, are gracefully represented round it. The God of wine stands quietly in the middle of his merry follovvers, leaning on a little Faun. Before him the old Silenus is seen staggering from drunkennes, supported by two of his companions. Of the Satyrs and Fauns, one is carrying a vase, another pours the wine from another vase ; some are playing on double pipes and on *siringae.* A goat hangs from a tree near an altar, on which stands a statue of Priapus. This interesting piece of sculpture, formerly stood in *Giustiniani's Gallery,* hence it bears its presents name of Giustiniani 's Well.

Before entering the Cabinet of the Masks in the passage leading to it:

422. Vase of oriental *colognino* alabaster standing on a pillar of *verde antico.* Found in the neighbourhood of *S. Carlo al Corso.* It stood on a cippus on which is a latin inscription referting to Liyilla the niece of Augustus as being buried within.

423-24. Faun holding grapes — Domitia.

425. Athletes victors in the games; a basrelief. It belonged to *Sir Thomas Jenkins.*

426. Basrelief with several figures of deities as the Sun, a Dioscur, Jupiter, Juno, Minerva, and the Fortun'.

CABINET OF MASKS.

Opening to the right side near the Giustia-
ni's Well, stands this beautiful and elegant Cabinet, the formation of which is due to the munificence of Pius VI. It is ornamented with eight
splendid columns and pilasters of that kind of alabaster called of *Monte Circeo*, each surmounted
with gilt capitals. Four red porphyry tables supported by bronze feet answer the purpose of seats.
The mosaic pavement, from which this Cabinet
takes its name, was brought from Adrian's villa.
and is divided into small squares or compartments
magnificently adorned with arabesques, and rich festoons of flowers. The middle compartment contains
some masks representing comic figures crowned
with laurel and ivy, a dragon the guardian of
the place , a panther , some festive emblems and
instruments of Bacchus, a landscape with a fountain and goats grazing. A female figure , holding
a sceptre. or pastoral staff, stands near the altar
and is supposed to be Libera or Ceres , the protectress of the flock. The various and brilliant colours of this beautiful mosaic , the smallness of
the pieces and good workmanship, make it produ-
ces almost the effect of a picture. The cieling is
finely decorated with oil paintings , by *Domenico
De Angelis*, the middle one representing the marriage of Bacchus and Ariadne celebrated by Hy-
men. The four laterals , Diana in the act of con-
templating her beloved Endymion; Paris refusing

the apple to Minerva and awarding it to Venus, the handsomest of the three goddesses, and lastly the beautiful Adonis standing before Venus, who sits near the trunk of a tree. An ancient frieze of marble representing Cupids adorns the cornice all round the lateral walls.

427. FEMALE DANCER or *Bacchante*. A life size statue in pentelic marble, found in the *Campania*, and purchased by Pius VI from the duchess of *Colubrano*. The delicacy of execution of the drapery, its admirable preservation, the truthfulness of the movements, gives it a claim to great merit, and makes it worthy to be ranged among the works of the highest order.

Let in the wall above:

428. A basreliefs allusive to Adrian's Apotheosis, representing the Emperor as standing in the company of Minerva Pacifera, with the figure of the greek sculptor, who made and dedicated the monument.

429. VENUS, in the act of coming out of the bath. A statue smaller than life, found at *Prato Bagnato* in the excavations of *Salona*, a farm lying on the right of the Praenestin Way. The graceful posture of this figure, imparts still more beauty to the general outline, and delicate limbs of the charming body. A vase for ointments, to which she is stooping, stands on one side, a small bracelet, the *spinkler* of Roman ladies, encircles her right arm. The name of *Bupalus* has been inscribed on the pedestal of the statue, after that of another found in the same place as the present, and alludes to the name of the sculptor of

the original, of which this is undoubtedly a copy.

430. *Set to the wall*: A basrelief representing
the SUN leaving in his *quadriga* the Cimmerian
grottoes, with Lucifer standing before him with
a raised torch, and one of the Dioscures. Two allegorical figures of the Sea and Heaven preceded
by those of Jupiter, Juno, Minerva, and Fortune,
adorn the other portion of this interesting basrelief.

431. Diana Lucifera, or light-bearer from the
torch she holds in her right hand. She is dressed in the Spartan costume, wearing the double
sistiles, opened on the left side.

432-444. *The two basre'iefs set in the wall above the iron-gratings, allude to other*: EXPLOITS
OF HERCULES. In the first N.ʳ 432. found at
Corcolle near *Praeneste*, Hercules is represented
slaughtering the lion of Nemea with a Nymph
seated above, as if to assist to the encounter. Af-
tèr comes the destruction of the seven-headed Ler-
næan Hydra by iron and fire; the bull of Eryman-
thum taken and carried off from Crete to Argos.
The Nymph of Apesanthos appears above seated
on a hill. Lastly, the slaying of the dragon, the
guardian of the Hesperides. On the other b. r.
N.ʳ 444. the hero is seen bringing alive before
Euristeus the swift stag of Ænoe. A Naias sits
on the adjoining Hill. The boar of Erymantheum
brought to Euristeus in the same manner. The
river has been introduced personified, under the
form of a nymph — The killing of the birds of
Stymphalus. On the other the hero is represented
cleansing the Augian stables by turning upon them

the river , whose waters are represented by the
figur · of the Nymph, standing above.

433. FAUNUS. This life-size statue represents
the rural god holding the pedum, fruits and grapes in the nebris, half thrown over his left shoulder. The right hand is raised to gather a bunch
of grapes, on which he is fondly looking. The
eyes formed of inlaid enamel , greatly serve te
heighten the expression. The castanets and *sy-
ringa*, the peculiar instruments of this god , are
hung on the trunk of the tree, against which he
is leaning. On account of the rich quality of marble, the *rosso antico*, in which it is sculptured ,
and the excellent manner it displays , it may be
reckoned among the most valuable monuments of
this collection. Found at *Tiroli* in *Adrian's Villa*.

434. Adventures of Hercules. A b. r. elegantly
divided into various compartments. In the central
ones, there are the images of Minerva, Mars, and
Amphytrion, ir connection with the adventures of
the hero , standing in the middle with the Scythian, who is teaching him the art of darting arrows. The equestrian and pedestrian figures , allude to the battle of the Thebans provoked by
the hero when a child, against Erginus the king
of Orchomenia. Found at *Palestrina* with other relating to the same subject.

435. Priest, cr Servant of Mithras. A statue erroneously taken for Paris by the sculptor who
on restoring it, added to it the apple. It undoubtedly represents one of the Geniuses os priests ,
who are often seen standing on the right and
left side of Mithraic sacrifices , the one generally

holding a flaming, the other an inverted torch , allusive perhaps to day and night, or more pro- bably representing the morning and evening stars.

436. A large cup in *rosso antico* beautifully wrought. It stands on a support of oriental ala- baster.

In the niche above:

437. An ancient mosaic brought from Adrian's villa , representing some scenes from the river Nile.

438. Minerva , an elegant statue , found in the villa of Cassius at *Tivoli.*

439. *Before the window: Sella Balnearia* or Ba- thing-seat, sculptured in a single block of ancient red , discovered outside the *Porta Maggiore.* It stands on a socket of rare ancient black marble.

440. A small basrelief in a very elegant style representing a Silenus and a dancing Faun pre- ceding Bacchus, who is supported by Ampelus.

441. *In the wall above:* Adventures of Hercules. A basrelief exhibiting various deeds of the hero. In three separate niches stand Minerva, Juno, and Bacchus. On one side Hercules is seen strangling the serpents sent against him when a child by Juno, whilst Alcmena and Amphytrio assist the exploit. On another , Hercules is playing on the lyre, in company of Linus his master, and the Muse Cal- liope. It was found as the others at *Corcolle , near Palestrina.*

442. GANIMEDES with the eagle. A statue smaller than life, found at *Quadraro,* a farm out- side the gate of *S. Giovanni.*

134

143. ADONIS. A statue of life size, remarkable
fos its good proportions and snowy polish, of the
purest kind of greek marble. Its high ideal expression of beauty , makes it a worthy rival of
the adjoining Venus. The melancholy look and
attitude of the figure, and the striking resemblance it bears to the beautiful son of Cyniras on some basreliefs, are the reasons because it was improperly restored as such , with the addition of
the javelin he holds in the right hand. But undoubtedly it is a copy of some statue of Apollo ,
represented as receiving the prayers and offerings
of mortals. It was dis·overed at *Centocelle* , outside the *Porta Maggiore.*

BALCONY OUT OF THE CABINET

445. *Above the entrance:* Priestess of Isis.

446. Sacrifice of Mithras, a basrelief set in the
wall.

448. *On the bracket:* Bust of Caracalla.

449. The Wolf giving suck to Romulus and Remus with ths shepherds Faustulus and Numitor,
a basrelief.

450. Thanksgiving to Æsculapius.

451. Bust unknown.

455. Bust of an Emperor.

Basreliefs set in the wall:

456-457. The races of the Circus — Deeds referring to the taking of Troy.

458-459. A Hunt — Mars surprising Rhea.

460-461. Birth and Death — Eteocles and Polynices.

462-463. Triumph of Bacchus and of Hercules — A sea-port.

On the bracket: Bust of an Emperor.

Basreliefs set to the wall.

464-465-467. A banquet — Priestess — Neptune.

468-469. Priest sacrificing on a tripod — Rural scene.

470. Bust unknown.

471-472. Bacchante — Ilia and Mars.

473-474. A prayer and sacrifice to a Deity,

475. Sacrifice of Mithras.

576. *On the bracket:* Antoninus Pius.

477-478. Ino suckling Bacchus. Found on the Caelian Hill — Birth of Hercules.

479-480. Female bust unknown — Bust unknown.

481. Bacchanalian found in the neighbourhood of Naples.

482. Nymphs wih Hercules, Diana and Sylvanus.

483. Bust of a Roman Emperor.

HALL OF THE MUSES.

A splendid Hall of a large octagono-rectangu-
lar form , built by *Simonetti* under Pius VII. It
is richly ornamented, by the munificence of Pius
IX, with modern decorations in the style of *Herculaneum*. Sixteen fine columns of *Carrara* marble with ancient corynthian capitals brought from
Adrian's Villa, are disposed round the Hall, and
support its large dome which is painted with
modern frescoes by *Cav. Conca*, representing both
mythological and poetical subjects, such as that in
the cieling: Apollo flaying Marsyas who is thied up
to a tree, while Olympus intercedes for his master. The other paintings in the compartment below
relate to the same subjects as: Apollo represented
with five Muses; Homer singing his poem. with
Minerva sitting on the clouds, and the Muses Ter-
phsycore and Clio, listening to him. The seven
wise men of Greece, with Mercury represented
above. Æschilus and Pindarus in the company of
Melpomene and Euterpe. In the lower corners ,
are four oil-paintings representing : Virgil with
the Muses Thalia and Calliope ; Homer and Calliope; *Ariosto* inspired by Apollo; lastly, *Tasso* in
the company of Minerva, and of the Muse Urania.
    The pavement is inlaid with ancient mosaic-
pieces, representing some very interesting theatrical groups rudely executed. They were disco-

vered at *Porcareccia*, eight miles from *Romœ* beyond *Porta Cavalleggeri*, near the site of the ancient *Lorium*. The one in the centre guarded .by a wooden balustrade, was discovered on the *Esquiline* in the gardens of the duke of *Sermoneta*. It represents a beautifully designed head of Medusa, surrounded by arabesques.

This Hall contains a very interesting collection of statues of Muses, Hermes of Greek philosophers, poets, and statesmen, nearly all discovered at *Tivoli* in the ancient villa of Cassius, now styled « *the Pianella of Cassius* » The statues were considered by *Visconti*, to be excellent copies after the originals of *Philiscus*, a Rhodian sculptor, which anciently stood in the *portico* of Metellus or Octavia. Almost all the objects of art in this Hall, are deserving of special note.

Entering from the Hall of Animals to the right side:

489. Set in the wall, above: PYRRIC DANCE. An interesting basrelief representing dances performed by some warriors, Corybantes and priests of Cybele, all naked, except the heads, covered with helmets. They are in the act of striking their swords against their shields alternately; but the swords are here wanting, as is usual in the representation of these exercises. The figures are one third the size of life. Though the basrelief may be supposed to belong to the better period of Greek art, notwithstanding it belongs to that of Adrian. Found a little outside of *Palestrina*.

490. DIOGENES THE CYNIC. An hermes-bust bearing his name, inscribed, in Greek characters

on the base. Plato named him « *the bad Socrates* » on account of the rudeness of his manners
and life.

491. SILENUS, A fine statue of life-size representing the forster-father of Bacchus crowned with ivy, wearing the tiger's skin thrown over a
part of his body, and fondly looking at the grapes which be holds in his left hand, while, he
presses their juice into a cup. It came from the
excavations of *Tor Cedrangola* near *Palestrina*.

492. HERMES OF SOPHOCLES the tragic poet. Found near the Temple of Peace.

Set in the left of the wall opposite:

493. THE BIRTH OF BACCHUS. A basrelief
Jupiter holding the sceptre in his left hand sits
on a rock. Mercury advancing towards him, is
hastening to receive the boy Bacchus in the nebrys he extends fowards him. Three goddesses,
perhaps Lucina, Proserpina, and Ceres, wrapped
in mantles, assist at the reception. This basrelief
though badly executed, is remarkable for its conception and antiquity, being supposed to belong to
the better period of the Republic. It probably served as a decoration to some temple. It was found
outside *Porta Portese*.

495. BACCHUS IN FEMALE ATTIRE. A life-
size statue. It was also better known as the
« *Hermaphroditus* » of *Villa Negroni* in which
it formerly stood. The head does not belong to
the figure, having been added to it afterwards.

496. HOMER. A terminal portrait-head exhibiting the traditional types and the sublime characteristics of the father of poetry. The hollow

eyes, refer to the description given of him by Pausanias, as a blind man. Smyrne, Colophon, Chion, Athens, Rhodes, Salamis, and Mytilene, contended for the honour of having given him birth.

« *Seven Grecian cities claimed the · poet dead, Through which the living Homer, begged his bread* ».

Within the octagon, on the right side of the Hall :

498. EPICURUS. Hermes-bust, found beyond *Porta Maggiore*.

499. MELPOMENE. The Muse of Tragedy is here represented in an heroic attitude as leaning against a rock, with her left foot raised, holding the poignard and the tragic herculean mask in her hands. Her abundant disheveled hair, falls in rich curls round her neck and shoulders. The bacchic crown on her head, denotes the rise of tragedy and drama, from the festivals and worship of Bacchus. Found in the *Villa* of *Cassius* at *Tivoli*.

500. ZENO, the Stoic philosopher. A hermes. bust.

501. Battle between Centaurs and Lapithae, a basrelief found outside the *Porta del Popolo*.

502. THALIA, a statue. The pastoral Muse who presided over Comedy, is sitting in a careless attitude on a rock, with crossed feet, adorned with sandals. She is crowned with a chaplet of ivy, and holds in both hands the *pedum* or pastoral staff, and the *tympanum*. The comic mask

lies beside her, on the rock. Found at *Tiroli*, as the preceding, in 1774.

503. ÆSCHINES, the rival of Demosthenes. His name is inscribed on his breast. Found at *Tiroli*,

504. URANIA, the Muse of Astronomy. This statue is easily recognised from the *stilus* and the celestial globe she holds in her hands. She is dressed in a large theatrical mantle, having the hair bound with a fillet. This statue formerly stood at *Velletri*, where it represented Fortune; afterwards it was restored as the celestial Muse with the addition of the globe, and *radius*. Discovered in *Adrian's villa*.

505. DEMOSTHENES. This beautiful portrait-head of the Greek orator, perfectly agrees with the expressive bust and statue of this celebrated man in the *Chiaramonti Corridor*, and *Braccio Nuovo*. On his left stands *AEschines*, his rival.

506. CLIO. According to Hesiod, Clio was the Muse who presided over History. She is here seated on a rock representing Parnassus, the head crowned with laurel, and a scroll of papyrus unfolded on her knees. Both the arms of this statue, are of modern restoration.

507. ANTISTHENES. A hermes. The chief and founder of the cynic sect appears here represented with distorted eyes, long disheveled hair, and neglected beard, in a form admirably suited to the subject. Found at *Tiroli* in the villa of Cassius.

508. POLYHYMNIA. A life-size statue. A garland of roses encircles the head of the Muse of Pantomime and Sacred Hymns. She is closely

covered with a large mantle falling richly folded at her feet. She seems deeply absorbed in meditation, as the Greeks usually represented her. The present statue bears a close resemblance to that of *Flora* which stands in the Museum of the Capitol. Found at *Tivoli* in 1774.

509. METRODORUS, the friend of Epicurus. A hermes-bust.

Going to the left hand of the Octagon:

510. ALCIBIADES, a portrait-hermes of the Athenian general and philosopher. Found in the villa *Fonseca*, on the Celian Hill.

511. ERATO. The muse of love, songs, and dances, is playing on the lyre made of the horns of oxen and tortoise-shell, like that of Apollo Cytharædus. This statue was designed by *Fontana*, a Roman sculptor. The head was supplied from another belonging to a statue of *Leda*.

512. EPIMENIDES, the Cretan philosopher. The closed eye-lids of this hermes bust, indicate the fabled sleep of fifty-seven years, into which it is said, he had fallen.

513. WRESTLING FAUNS AND CENTAURS. A b. r. found with the one opposite near the *Porta del Popolo*, in the *Odescalchi* grounds.

514. CALLIOPE. The finest and the most admired statue of the present collection of Muses, representing that of Epic poetry, seated on a rock, as if meditating, with the wax-tablets *«pugilares»* on her knees. The *stylus* alone is here wanting. The arrangement of the drapery is so perfect, that nothing remains to be desired to add grace and beauty to the statue.

515. SOCRATES, an authentic portrait-bust of the philosopher, who although remarkably ugly, of features was reputed the wisest and most virtuous of mortals. Were it not that we find his name inscribed in Greek characters on the bust, we might mistake, it for a Silenus, from the close resemblance they bear to one another. This may be most probably a copy of the original by *Lysippus* erected to his memory, after his violent and cruel death.

516. APOLLO CYTHARÆDUS, Harplayer. The god of Poetry, the inspired leader of the Muses is here represented in an animated attitude, wearing a long robe, and a flowing mantle. The head is crowned with a wreath of laurel. With his right hand he touches with a *plectrum* the harmonious strings of his lyre, on one side of which is a basrelief, representing Marsyas fastened to a tree. This statue admirable on account of its delicacy of sculpture, according to *Visconti*, is the best known of the antique statues of this god as *Musageles*. It is supposed to be a copy of that celebrated original statue of Apollo Harp-player by *Thymarchides* or rather as some more probably assert, after the original of *Scopas*. The statue of *Thymarchis* stood along with the nine muses of Phyliscus, and those of Diana and Latona, in the *Portico* of *Octavia*. It probably served as a model to the Emperor Nero, whose foolish ambition was to be represented in such attitude, on his coins. It was discovered at *Tivoli* in the « *Pianella of Cassius* ».

517. THEMISTOCLES. A fine helmeted hermes bust of the illustrious Athenian general and statesman.

518. TERPSICORE, one of the nine sisters, who presided over dances, and sacred lyric poetry. She is represented crowned with laurel, and playing on the double horned lyre, as we see her on the frescoes of Herculaneum. This statue is a copy of the renowned original by *Phyliscus* which as Pliny says, stood in the *Portico* of *Octaria*.

519. ZENO, the Eleatic philosopher, A hermes· bust.

520. EUTERPE. The Muse of harmonious songs and melodies, sits on a rock like her companion Erato, holding a *tybia* in her right hand, which is of modern restoration. Her modest and simple garnment, is elegantly fastened with a gem on her right shoulder. This statue was long admired in the *Lancellotti* palace. It is of Pentelic marble.

In the restibule opening to the Round Hall:

521. Bust of Euripides the tragic-greek poet.

522. Nuptial feasts, a basrelief.

523. ASPASIA, the wife of Pericles, whose influence , was so strongly exercised over his mind, as to lead him to the unrivalled height of glory he acquired. Her name is inscribed lower down the pedestal of this bust. It was discovered at *Castro Nuovo*, a village near *Civilarecchia*.

524. SAPPHO, a statue representing the poetess of Mytilene seated on a rock, which repre-

sents Parnassus, because from her poetical genius, she has deserved the glorious name of the tenth Muse.

Right side set to the wall:

525. PERICLES, helmeted hermes-bust of the famous ruler of Athens, who did so much to embellish that city, and who deserved to have given his name to the golden age of Greece, in which Phidias and Praxiteles lived. His name, as well that of his father Xanthyppus, and of his fatherland, are inscribed on the breast in greek characters.

526. Solon. A headless hermes found at Tivoli.

527. Pithagoras. A headless hermes.

528. The Rape of Proserpina, a b. r.

In the arch before entering the Round Hall:

Set to the wall above the entrance to the Circular Hall, is a Latin inscription which refers to the recovery of the objects of art of the present collection after their removal to Paris, made by Pius VII.

529. BIAS of PRIENE. A portrait bust bearing the name of this celebrated lawgiver, and his favourite maxim « *Multi homines mali* » « There are many bad men » Found at *Tivoli in Adrian's Villa.*

530. LYCURGUS. Life-size bearded statue of the great Spartan legislator represented in a severe costume, viz, with the simple cloak. With the index of his right hand, he points to his eye as indicating the insult received from Aleander. It was discovered at *Civitavecchia.*

531. PERIANDER. Hermes-bust bearing the name of the philosopher and his special motto « *Nothing is impossible to an industrious man.* » Found at *Tivoli.*

532. Medallion representing Juno.

533. Minerva, a statue.

534. Head of Medusa, a b. r.

In the niche:

535. Mnemosine, the mother of the Muses, a very rare statue. It is very interesting, and deserves a peculiar interest of the Archeologist. It stands over a sarcophagus representing the Muses of Comedy and Tragedy.

536. A Festoon made of oak-leaves.

ROTUNDA *or* CIRCULAR HALL

Built by Pius VI from the designs of the architect Simonetti, who took the idea of its form, from the dome of the Pantheon. It was purposely erected, to serve as a convenient and worthy receptacle for the large and magnificent basin in red porphyry, forty five feet in circumference, found in the Baths of Diocletian. This splendid Hall is tastefully decorated with ten fluted pillars of *Carrara* marble, with carved capitals. It has been greatly enriched nnder the present pontif PIUS IX, with gildings and wall paintings, but particularly by the colossal bronze statue of Hercules. The largest and most magnificent mosaic known, composes the floor. It is divided into concentric bands, by festoons of flowers, fruits and masks. Each band contains representations of combats between Centaurs and Lapithae, Nereids, and Nymphs carried on the backs of Tritons, and various other fabulous sea monsters. In the centre between the lions head of gilt bronze which support the grand basin, we see a colossal modern head of Medusa. The border which fills the passage round the hall, is made of black and white mosaic pieces, found at *Scrofano*, representing some of the adventures of Ulysses, Neptune with his sea-horses, and other fabulous monsters. Colossal and semicolossal statues, are tastefully arranged within the corresponding niches with a rich series of busts, which stand on porphyry columns, imparting a peculiar beauty to the excellent architecture, and grandeur of the Hall. It is 61. feet in diameter.

On each side of the Entrance :

537-338. TRAGEDY AND COMEDY, two colossal hermes sculptured by Roman artists, in the finest Greek style. Their execution seems probably to refer to the time of Adrian. They were brought here from the villa of that Emperor, where they anciently stood as an ornament to the entrance of the theatre. On looking at them we immediately perceive the beautiful contrast between the gayful and intellectual expression of the Hermes of Comedy, and the majestic severity and melancholy sadness of the other, the Tragedy.

539. *On the right hand :* JUPITER. Colossal bust. It is the most beautiful representation of all hnown statues and busts of the father of the

gods. The benign yet majestic expression of the the features, is the true ideal type of the greek divinities. It is an excellent copy of the Jupiter by Phidias, which is said to have perished at *Bizantium* during a conflagration, with many other masterpieces of art. It seems to be of a later date than the time of Alexander. It came from the ruins of *Otricoli.*

540. ANTINOUS, colossal statue. The head is beautifully adorned with a rich and full crown of flowers, from the middle of which, springs an opened lotus-flower. The ample drapery is of modern execution. It was removed here from the *Lateran Museum.*

541. FAUSTINA THE ELDER, the wife of Antoninus Pius. A colossal bust, discovered at *Pantanello* in the *Villa Adrianea.*

542. VEILED AUGUSTUS. A life-size statue in greek marble, remarkable for its well arranged drapery. The emperor is represented personified as a Genius, standing closely veiled in the sacerdotal habit of *Pontifex Maximus*, in the act of sacrificing, holding the *patera* in one hand, and a *cornucopiae* in the other. It originally stood in the *Colubrano* palace at *Naples.*

543. ADRIAN, a very interesting colossal head in pentelic marble found in the last century within the inclosure of Adrian' s Mausoleum , now *Castle St. Angelo.* It is supposed it had belonged to a colossal statue of the same Emperor, which stood in the vestibule of his tomb.

In the central niche:

544. THE Mastai HERCULES. An interesting
antique statue of colossal proportions in gilt bronze. It represents the demi-god in all his power-
ful strenght , leaning on his club. A lion's skin
is thrown over his left arm. In one hand he holds
the apples of the garden of the Hesperides. Although injured somewhat by time, it still deserves a good deal of merit as a work of art. The
feet and club have been skilfully restored by *Sig.
Tenerani.* It was discovered in 1864 on restoring
the foundations of the *Biscioni* [1] Palace which belonged to *Righetti,* of whom it was purchased by
Pius IX for a sum exceeding 45,000 *scudi.* This
rightly deserved it the name of its Generous Pur-
chaser.

545. ANTINOUS, Adrian's fauvourite, is here
represented as an Egyptian deity, as we may con-
clude from the falling of the hair over the shoulders , and his issuing from the large leaves of
a lotus-flower which surround his breast. As such
he may have been worshipped at Antinopolis , a
city which bore his name , and was dedicated to
him as an inferior deity. It was discovered in the
Villa Fede at *Tivoli.*.

456. CLAUDIUS. A very remarkable colossal
statue. The Emperor is represented after his apotheosis under the attributes of Jupiter, half draped, the head encircled with the civic crown of
oak-leaves, the *patera*, in the act of receiving the
worship and thanksgiving from his subjects.

[1] This palace stands near the *Piazza* of *Campo di Fiori.* It
covers a portion of the area, where stood the large theatre of
Pompey, and its magnificent porch.

Both the right and left arms and hands with a portion of the drapery and the eagle , are modern additions by *Galli*.

It came from the most recent excavations of *Civita Lavinia*.

On the pedestal of this statue are sculptured on basreliefs , games of the Circus, performed by Cupids.

547. COLOSSAL HERMES BUST representing the OCEAN or some another Sea-divinity, perhaps *Glaucus*. In the luxuriant hair, fishes, waves, dolphins, sea-shells, vine-leaves, and grapes, are beautifully interwoven together, undoubtedly a tipe of the fertile shores of *Baiae and Pozzuoli* near *Naples*, where it was found. As a good model of the sculptures of *Magna Graecia*, it claims our highest consideration.

548. NERVA. Sitting colossal statue of this good Emperor, represented crowned with a bronze wreath of oak-leaves. The countenance is majestic , the lower limbs are covered with a graceful drapery , the upper part of the body is bare. The head bears a perfect likeness of the emperor. This statue was discovered near the walls between *S. Giovanni in Laterano*, and *Sta. Croce in Gerusalemme*. On the pedestal which was found at Ostia is a very interesting basreliefs representing *Vulcan*, who persuades Juno, to resign herself to Jupiter's counsels. Discovered at *Ostia*.

549. Colossal majestic bust of JUPITER SERAPIS, wearing the *modius*, a corn measure. The seven rays which formerly adorned the fillet round tha head, are now wanting. It vas found at *Co-*

lombaro on the Appian Way, at a short distance
from the ancient *Bovillae*.

550. JUNO BARBERINI, so styled by *Cardina-
le Francesco Barberini* who discovered it on the
Viminal, near the *Olympian Baths*, now the church of *S. Lorenzo in Panisperna*. This magnificent colossal statue is one of the most perfect specimens of antique sculpture. Its beautiful finish,
the delicacy and grandeur of its execution, its ar-
tificial arrangement of drapery, the noble expression of the head, all make it a worthy representation of such a goddes. It is considered a very
fine copy of the celebrated work of Praxiteles which
according to Pausanias was admired in the
temple of Plateae, dedicated to that goddes, and
which afterwards was supposed had perished at
Bizantium during a conflagration. Young artists
will find in this masterpiece of sculpture a beautiful ideal in marble.

551. CLAUDIUS. A well preserved colossal bust
found at *Otricoli*. The head adorned with the civic crown of oak leaves, is turned towards the
right side, and gives us a more flattering portrait
of this Emperor, than that attributed to him by
historians.

552. JUNO LANUVINA. The Goddes is here represented in the warlike Pelasgic costume, covered with the goat's skin which is gathered round
her breast. The costume, according to the description given by Cicero, is the same one, in which
she was represented on the ancient roman coins,
as also that, under which she was worshipped in
her sanctuaries of Rome, and of the city of *Lanu-*

vium. The present one is supposed to have belonged to her temple on the Palatine. It is sculptured in greek marble. Both the arms, the spear and shield, she bears in the hands, a portion of the legs, the pointed sandals, and the serpent her usual symbol, are all modern additions. The statue itself is not much, as a work of art; its singular costume however attracts our attention. It formerly stood in the *Paganica Palace*.

553. PLOTINA, colossal bust, exhibiting the characteristic features of the wife of Trajan. The careful head-dress, is the same in this bust, as that on her imperial coins. Found on the *Celium*.

554. COLOSSAL HEAD OF JULIA PIA the second wife of the emperor Septimius Severus, discovered beyond *Porta S. Giovanni* in the farm of *Quadraro*.

555. CERES. A large colossal statue in pentelic marble of the goddess of agriculture represented holding ears of corn. It is valuable on account of the simple yet excellent arrangement of the drapery. It formerly stood in the *Palazzo della Cancelleria*.

556. PUBLIUS ELVIUS PERTINAX, the wise successor of Commodus, represented at the age of seventy. A very expressive colossal bust.

In the middle of the Hall:

557. LARGE BASIN, in red porphyry. It measures 46 feet in circumference. It was given to Julius III by *Ascanius Colonna*, and was discovered in front of the Baths of Diocletian.

HALL OF THE GREEK CROSS.

To this Hall we pass, through a large wooden portal finely decorated with gildings and lions heads. At each side of the entrance, are two colossal statues of *Telamones*, masterly sculptured in the Romano-Egyptian style. The Greeks introduced *Typhons* into their architecture to support buildings like *Athlantes*; similar supports were used by the Romans, known under the names of *Telamones*. They support like Caryatides huge columns on which rests a majestic entablature of white marble, bearing in bronze characters the name of Pius VI, the founder of this Hall.

This entablature is surmounted by a valuable basrelief, representing two gladiators fighting with wild-beasts. The statues as well as the bases, are of a beautiful kind of egyptian granite. They formerly were in Adrian's villa, where, perhaps they adorned the entrance of the « *Canopus* ».

The Hall was constructed by *Michael Angelo Simonetti*. It is divided into four compartments, forming a *Greek Cross*, hence its name. It was intended purposely for the two porphyry sarcophagi, placed in the compartments on the right and left. In the marble pavement are fine specimens of ancient coloured mosaics. The one before the colossal door represents a *Faun* or a *Bacchus* watering a flower with his favourite liquor. It was found at *Falerona* in the *Marca d'Ancona*. The most esteemed of the mosaics, is the splendid circular one in the middle of the Hall,

154

which is enclosed by a wooden balustrade. It was discovered at *La Rufinella*, the well known villa of Cicero , in the year 1741. Among various circles of festoons, arabesques, and symbolical figures, there is in the centre a beautiful representation of a bust of Minerva with the ægis, the head of Medusa on the breast, the helmet and shield. Twelve planets, with the various phases of the Moon are exhibited in the circular belt. The last segment of the circle on which are Gorgon's masks , as well as the blue and white figures of Telamons, are its only modern additions. The composition is admirable, on account of the brightness and harmony of the various colours.

The most remarkable objects worthy of attention are two magnificent SEPULCHRAL URNS or SARCOPHAGI of an extraordinary size , cut in a single block of red Egyptian porphyry.

Set to the wall:

558. Chimera, a basrelief. *See N.ᵉʳ 596.*

559- AUGUSTUS. A very fine half-draped statue remarkable for its good style of sculpture and the likeness it bears to Napoleon the first. The head which never was separated from the bust , enhances its value. It formerly stood in the *Verospi Palace.*

5560-561. Female bust — Mercury the protector of trade, a statue.

562. Youthful Head.

563. Cieling sculptured in marble. *See N.ᵉʳ 568.*

564. LUCIUS VERUS. A statue larger than life , discovered in the forum of Præneste. On its pedestal there is a basrelief, representing Hercu-

les dining, wearing the *scyphus* or *cantharus*, whilst a child offers him a loaf of bread.

565. Hercules, a statue standing on a cippus erected to *Titus Staberius by Staberia his mother*.

566. That one standing to the right of the entrance before the window, served as a tomb, and contained the bones of Sta. Costantia, the friend of Agnes, and the daughter of Costantine the Great. It formerly stood in the church supposed to have been erected as a Mausoleum to Costantine and his family, adjoining the Church of St. Agnes, in the Nomentan Way. It is ornamented with representations in basrelief of winged boys or Cupids gathering grapes in allusion to the mystic vine, an emblem commonly seen in Christian inscriptions, as well as sheep, lambs, pea-cocks grotesque works, festoons, and arabesques. The rude style in which they are sculptured, indicates the decline of art under Costantine.

A.566-567. Sarcophagus — Priestess of Ceres, found on the Cassian Way.

568. *See N.ʳ 565*.

569-571. EUTERPE — CLIO. Semicolossal statues of the two sister Muses. The one was brought here from the theatre of *Otricoli*, where it served as a decoration; the other came from *Roma Vecchia*.

570. Bust of Faustina, found at *Ostia*.

Set above in the wall:

572. DIDIUS JULIANUS. Very rare bust of the successor of Publius Helvius Pertinax, well known for having purchased the Roman empire from the

Prætorian guards. It closely resembles his ancient coins.

573. A very interesting basrelief representing some Muses. *See N°°. 580.*

574. VENUS OF CNIDOS. A statue larger than life, the most perfect copy known of the original by *Praxiteles,* so celebrated throughout the world, and which was lost in a conflagration at *Bizantium,* at the close of the Fourth Century. An air of majesty and loveliness distinguishes the charming features of the Goddess. The bronze drapery, afterwards added, conceals much of the fair proportions of the lower part of her limbs. Only the left and right forearm are its modern restorations.

575. Head of Adrian found at *Ostia.*

576-577. Genii, Faun, and Bacchantes standing around a *cratere.* Basreliefs.

578-579. Before the large staircase there are TWO SPHINXES in Egyptian granite. The one was discovered in the vineyard of Pope Julius II. outside the *Porta del Popolo*; the other on making the staircase of St. Peter's.

Set in the pavement, between these two fabulous animals, there is a beautiful basket of flowers in mosaic, discovered in the ruins of *Roma Vecchia* four miles from *Porta Maggiore, on the Appian Vay.*

In the niche, opposite the statue of Venus:

580. See N.°° 573.

581. Head of Trajan found in the excavations of *Ostia.*

582. APOLLO PALATINUS. A valuable statue of the renowned original of *Scopas* which stood in the temple dedicated to this god on the Palatine Hill. The god is represented in the act of playing on the lyre. It is erroneously styled the Muse Erato. It was brought from the *Quirinal.* On the pedestal of the statue, there is a female head in high relief.

583. Marcus Aurelius, a semicolossal head, from *Ostia.*

684. Small statue of Diana chasing.

585. Marciana, the sister of Trajan.

586. Winged Victory, a b. r.

587. Euterpe. A statue larger than life. Lower down the pedestal Meneläus is represented dedicating to Apollo the arms of Euphorbus.

588. Roman Matron. The cippus is sacred to *Hospiti Leonidiniano by Libertus Polibius.*

590. Beardless Statue of a man of life-size. It stands on a cippus, on which is an inscription dedicated to *Syphax* the King of Numidia, who vanquished by Scipio, was led to Rome to adorn his triumph. The Latin inscription relates to the death of this unhappy king, which happened in the Tiburtine territory, where he was banished in the 47th year of his age, after eleven months of captivity.

A. 590-591. See N.ᵉʳ 536.

592. *In the niche*: Orator in the act of haranguing; it was brought from *Otricoli.*

593-594. Male bust — Small statue of Fortune.

595. Antoninus Pius, a colossal head found at *Ostia.*

596. See N.ʳʳ 558.

597. *In the niche*: AUGUSTUS. A statue of the same size as the one opposite, brought from the *Ocriculan Colony*. The emperor is represented all veiled, as *Pontifex Supremus*, holding the *patera* in his right hand, in the act of offering a sacrifice. The statue of Livia his wife, which stands in the Gallery of the Statues, was brought from the same place, as the present.

In the niches adjoining the iron grating of the Garden :

598-599. Athlete — Hercules, statues.

On the first landing of the magnificent stair- case, opposite the entrance to the Egyptian Mu- seum, in the recess of the window, stands a co- lossal reclining statue, representing the river.

600. TIGRIS. This remarkable piece of sculpture was restored in the head, right arm and left hand by *Michael Angelo Buonarroti*. It served as a de- coration to some fountain, the water issuing from the amphora the figure holds in its right hand. So majestic and strongly expressive a figure, re- minds us of the renowned statue of *Moses* by the same *Michael Angelo*, which now stands in *S. Pie- tro in Vincoli*, and also of that of the Nile, in the « *Braccio Nuovo* ».

MARBLE STAIRCASE

This magnificent Staircase was erected by *Simonetti*, the architect of the Hall, under Pius VI. It is richly adorned with steps, *cimase*, entabla- tures in white marble, bronze balustrades, and columns of Oriental, granite, *breccia*, and porphyry. One of the four flights into which it is divided, leads to the Vatican Garden and also communicates by a iron-grating with the opposite north arm of the Library. On ascending to the first landing we reach the entrance to the Egyptian Museum. By two lateral arms we ascend, and reach the hall of the *Biga*, and the extensive corridors ot the Hall of the *Candelabra*, of the *Tapestries* and *Geographical Maps*. The third spacious flight, by which from the landing of the Biga, we ascend to the Etruscan Museum, is grandly decorated by ten fine columns. The four sustaining the vaults, are of a *corallina breccia*, four others of *Breccia* of *Cori*, and lastly those which adorn the opening in the form of a balcony on the Hall of Greek Cross, are of a very rare black porphyry, probably the only ones known any where of the same material.

They were found at the *Tre Fontane*, outside the *Gate of St. Paul*. The double handled Oval Vase (606.) of the rarest *plasma* granite is richly decorated with masks of Silenus. It stands on a cippus, on which are engraved the arms of Pius VI, by whom the present *Loggia* was expressly made, in order to afford a better view of the rich mosaic pavement of the Greek Hall, and of the covers of the porphyry sepulchral urns.

To the right side, close to the entrance of the Etruscan Museum:

601. TRIPOD in highrelief exhibiting the combat of Hercules with the sons of Hippocoon, some of whom have fallen to the ground, while others

attack the hero with their clubs. This rare and remarkable monument is supposed to have served as a lustration vase in the vestibule of some temple dedicated to Hercules. Its state of preservation is excellent. It was discovered in the *Vigna Casali*, on the *Appian Way*.

· *Set in the lateral wall :*

602. Two winged Victories supporting a medallion with the portrait bust of a matron.

603. Fragment of a Sarcophagus. The subject of this relief is very interesting, as it exhibits a scene from the life of *Medea*. The sorceress is represented in the act of delivering to her sons the poisoned gifts, viz the veil and crown to be presented to her rival *Glauce*. The latter is represented seated on a throne, surrounded by her nurse and some of her attendants. She looks unsuspiciously at the presents brought her by the children, the innocent executors of the cruel vengeance taken by their mother on the unhappy rival. Of the two other figures, that one standing behind Glauce holding poppies in her hands, alludes to the Genius of Death, the other may represent Creon, the father of Glauce, lamenting the fate of his unfortunate daughter.

In the niches:

604. Cybele enthroned between two lions.

605. *In the niche:* Dacian Prisoner represented with a long hairy head dress, clothed with a skin, having the hands tied behind his back.

Descending from this floor to the second, on the right side we enter the :

This beautiful octangular Hall was erected by *Camporesi*, under Pius VI. The well lighted *cupola* which is a miniature of the Pantheon, is adorned with *rosoni in stucco*, and is supported by eight fluted carystian columns, with eagles and festoons of marble in the partitions, splendidly wrought.

In the pavement inlaid with various kinds of marble, is the arms of the family of Pius VI. On account of its elevated position it commands a view of the greater portion of the Vatican gardens, the mediæval walls of Leo IV, and one of the best prospects of the dome of St. Peter's. The hall was expressly made to contain the fine monument of the *Biga*, from which it takes its name.

608. *In the niche:* INDIAN BACCHUS, or SARDANAPALUS, the king of Assyria, so celebrated for his luxury and effeminacy. The figure is enveloped in a long falling mantle, on the border of which, his name is written in greek characters. The long beard, and the sceptre he holds in the right hand, give an expression of greater majesty to the countenance. Found with the Cariatides of Villa Albani in a niche near *Monte Porzio*, where Lucius Verus is known had a villa.

609. The sarcophagi placed under the niches where are the statues of *Phocion, the Veiled Roman, and the Sardanapalus*, were found in different places, viz in the *Catacombs of St. Sebastian*, and in the *Vigna Moroni*. They exhibit interesting scenes in alto rilievo of the GAMES OF THE CIRCUS performed by charioteers, under the form of winged boys, or Cupids. Some are represented contesting for the prize, others have fallen from their chariots, lastly the bravest reach the desired *meta*, and are honoured by the victor's crown.

610. BACCHUS. A statue of life size, restored in the limbs. The torso is a refined specimen of Greek Art. The long hair so celebrated by ancient poets, falls in rich curled masses over the shoulders.

611. ALCIBIADES. The Athenian general, so renowned, both for his beauty and military skill is represented in a heroic attitude, grasping a sword, and pressing a helmet with the right foot, as if in the act of defending it. The figure is full of life, and displays extraordinary energy and action. We may suppose this statue to be a copy of the original by Nycerates, which was erected to the hero by the Romans in the *Comitium*. The present one was found on the *Celian Hill*, in the *Villa Fonseca*.

612. ROMAN PERSONAGE represented entirely veiled, holding a patera, in the act of offering a sacrifice. This statue larger than life is enveloped in a long falling mantle, on the border of which, his name is written in Greek

characters. The long beard, and the sceptre he holds in the right hand, give an expression of greater majesty to the countenance. Found with the Cariatides of Villa Albani in a niche near *Monte Porzio,* where Lucius Verus is known had a Villa.

613. *See N.* 609.

614. Apollo Cytharædus. A statue found near the *Piazza di S. Silvestro in Capile.*

In the next niche :

615. DISCOBOLUS IN REPOSE, a life size statue, one of the best imitations of the celebrated original of *Naukides.* The gamester has been represented in a very simple and naturally expressive attitude, with the right foot and leg forward, looking at the discus, before throwing it. The good preservation and exquisite beauty of style of this statue, affords us a specimen of first class Greek sculpture. It was discovered by *Gavin Hamilton* at *Colombaro,* a farm two leagues distant from Rome, near the Appian Way, where there was a summer-house of the Emperor Gallienus.

616. PHOCION. A life-size statue of the renowned Athenian general and philosopher. He is represented in the heroic costume of a warrior, wearing only a rough chlamys, a helmet, and legs and feet bare. It was discovered in the *Via Rasella* near the *Gentili Palace* at the foot of the Quirinal, in the place where the temple of Archemorus anciently stood.

617. See N.* 609.

618. DISCOBOLUS IN ACTION. A remarkable statue executed after the renowned original in

bronze of *Myron*, of which *Lucianus* and *Quin-
tilianus* speak. The figure appears full of physical energy and action, the foot advanced, and the
body thrown forward in the act of hurling the
discus. It will not be here out of place to give a
short sketch of this renowned game. The discus
was one of the five gymnastic exercises, namely,
wrestling, running, javelin throwing, and discus.
The latter was formed of a thin plate of stone,
iron, or copper. It was used by Romans and Greeks
in their exercises, and the Discobolus who threw
it the farthest, received as a prize a fillet, with
which he was decorated. This game was the most
dangerous of all, for by it Perseus killed his grand-
father, and Hyacintus lost his life at the hands of
Apollo. It was common throughout all Greece at
the time of the siege of Troy. The name of *Myron*
is engraved on the trunk of the tree against which
the statue leans, as also as a portion of the strigil. It was found at *Adrian's Villa* towards the
close of the Sixteenth Century.

619. ROMAN CHARIOTEER, or AURIGA OF
THE CIRCUS, dressed in his costume, the body
and thigh adorned with a corslet and bands. In
the left hand he holds a portion of the reins,
which he has cut with the curved knife fastened
to the bands of the corslet. The branch of a palm
in his right hand, is a token of the victory gained in the games. The greater portion of this
statue is modern. It came from the *Villa Negroni*.

620. The upper niche contains a draped statue
of a philosopher holding a scroll. He is supposed

to be SEXTUS of CHERONEA the master and friend of M. Aurelius, and uncle of Plutarch.

621. SARCOPHAGUS, exhibiting in basreliefs the fatal chariot-race of Pelops, and Œnomaüs, a subject from the tragedies of *Sophocles* and *Euripides*. On it we see the king Œnomaüs in the act of being thrown from the chariot by Pelops, who afterwards becomes the husband of Hyppodamia, the daughter of Œnomaüs, who together whit Myrtilus the charioteer and Pelops, caused the death of her father, and the triumph of her lover. She and her nurse, appear on one side evidently sorry, and apprehensive of the consequences of their rash deed. A sort of milestone marks the *meta*, and a crowd of spectators stands on the right side awaiting the result of the race.

622. Diana. A small statue in a short hunting dress. She is in the act of starting the chase, attended by one of her faithful greyhounds; discovered near the « *Tempio della Pace* ». Undoubtedly it is a copy of some renowned Greek original.

623. BIGA. This valuable piece of art, anciently stood in some temple dedicated to the Sun, as a votive offering to that deity. Only the body of the chariot is ancient. It was presented to Pius VI. by the Canons of St. Mark's church of Rome, in whose choir it stood, and served for a long time as an episcopal chair, during the celebration of High Mass. The reins, the pole, and the horses with the exception of the, torse of the right one, (a gift of *Prince Borghese* to Pius VI,) are modern additions by *Franzoni.* The chariot and the

pole are adorned with beautiful carvings and arabesques, acanthus, flowers poppies, ears of corn, laurel-branches, and ribbons. The horses are of excellent workmanship, and seem as if ready to start on their course. This beautiful work of art, adds greater splendour to the architectural proportions of the Hall.

GALLERY

OF THE VASES AND CANDELABRA.

From the Hall of the Biga we come to a
large corridor, known under this denomination. It
is divided into six sections by fine columns of *gri-
gio marble*. The first one is decorated with pillars of alabaster from *la Tolfa*, near *Civilavecchia*.
Each section contains a particular series of monuments of ancient art, arranged on both sides,
consisting of sarcophagi, cups, crateres, arae, vases, statues, mosaics, frescoes, and several finely
sculptured candelabra. This collection though not
very well arranged, yet claims our attention for
its rich variety of coloured stones, and also for
the artistic value of some sculptures.

First Division.

Beginning on the right :
1. VASE with handles of a rare *breccia verde*,
of Egypt. It stands on a half pillar of red porphyry.

2-66. *At each side near the grating :* TWO
TRUNKS OF TREES supporting nests, in which
are five little children, beautifully executed. On
the base of the one is an Egyptian hawk sculptured in b. r.

3-4. Colossal foot — Torse of a Faun.

5. Headless draped figure.

6. JASO, in the act of putting a sandal on his foot; a graceful small statue.

7-8-9-10-11. Torse of Bacchus — Foot of a statue — Torsi — Torse standing on an altar.

19-13. Faun — Small torse.

14. Vase of red porphyry, put on a small pillar of Egyptian granite.

15-16. Hermes with heads of Silvanus.

17-18. Vases of *nero* and *bianco* oriental granite.

19. Rare and beautiful statue of a CHILD represented in the act of playing at the ancient game of *capila and navim*, commonly called by our boys « *Arma e Santo* » He hastens curiously to look forward at the fallen money, to find if it represents the image of *Janus Bifrons* the *capila*, or *navim*, the ship.

20. OVAL SARCOPHAGUS of a Roman Child whose figure appears lying down on the lid, dressed in a philosophical *pallium*, and holding a volume in its hands. In the front of the sarcophagus we see in b. r. the figure of the same boy, surrounded by the Genii of the Muses. Found in the Catacombs of *Ciriacus* on the Salarian Way.

21. OVAL VASE of a very fine rose alabaster. It stands on a pilaster of *cipollino marble*. Found in the *Roman Forum*.

Left and right side:

22-23. Julia Soemia, the mother of Elagabalus-Telamon.

24. Torso standing on a pillar of *bigio* fluted marble.

25. Torso in greek marble.

26-27. Fragments of a colossal foot and toe in flowered alabaster. They perhaps belonged to some gigantic statue, which anciently served to adorn the front façade of some temple. Discovered near the *Colosseum*.

28-29-30. Hercules — Two small torsi.

31-35. TWO ELEGANT CANDELABRA. On one of their triangular bases are engraved a dancing Faunus, and a Bacchante, the other exhibits the myth of Apollo flaying Marsyas, with the figures of Olympus and the Scythian. Found on the *Celium*. Both stand on altars, adorned with Egyptian divinities in basrelief, discovered at *Otricoli*.

32-33-34. Fragment of a statue — *Cratere* of Egyptian granite, on a pillar of *cipollino*.

36-37-38. Hermes with a Lion's skin—Torse—Bacchus.

39-40. Torso — Head of a Lion in *alabastro di Montallo*.

41. Foot with buskin in *florito* alabaster.

42-43· Castor and Pollux, fragments of statues—Torso of a Faun.

44-45. Hercules — Female Faun.

46-56. Two oval vases of a singular *Genoese and Theban Serpentino*.

47. Unknown statue.

48. CINERARY URN with its cover, of rarest Egyptian *granitello*. It stands on a pillar of *giallo antico*.

49. CHILD, in the act of plucking a bunch of

grapes. A very expressive little statue. It came from *Orvieto*.

50. Vase of *serpentino bigio porphyry* of Etruscan form.

51 Torso of Cupid.

52. FAUNUS. Recumbent statue sculptured in green basalt, a marble very hard to be worked. It represents a drunken Faun crowned with pine-leaves and apples, sleeping ou its nebrys.

52-54-55. Torso of an Athlete and Faun — Diana.

56-46. Oval Vases with double handles of *Verde Plasma, and Genoese Serpentina*.

57-58. Genius — Child

59-60. Torso of an Athlete put on a cinerary urn.

61-62-63. Fragments of statues.

64-65. Small torse — Faun, a seated figure.

67-68. A Foot — Hercules.

69. VASE of the most rare *Lysimaco jasper*, with spots of *lapislazzuli*. It stands on a pillar of *Breccia of Aleppo*.

Second Division.

To the right and left side:

70-123. Two handled vases of a *serpentino porphyry*.

71-72. Child representing Winter — Vase ornamented with ivy-leaves.

73. Hercules child strangling the serpents, a small statue erected by *Ulpius Doriphorus* a medecin and *Libertus of Augustus*.

74. FAUN extracting a thorn from the foot of a Satyr, who distracted by the pain, forgets his bag, from which the wine is flowing out. A small and expressive group. It served to ornament some fountain, in the *Mattei Villa*.

75. HANDLED CUP of *ligrato marble*, a gift of Pope Pius IX. It stands on a round support, having the form of a tripod.

76. VASE in the form of a stove, of beautiful oriental alabaster. The tripod on which it stands is ornamented with lion's paws, and heads of Hercules.

77. See N.ᵉʳ 72.

78-79. Genius of Summer — Vase of white marble beautifully adorned with scenic masks by *Franzoni*.

80. Cupid.

81. *In the niche:* DIANA OF EPHESUS *or* MULTIMAMMEA. A statue larger than life. The goddess stands here in the costume in which she was worshipped in her renowned temple of Ephesus. Her breasts are sixteen in number, in allusion perhaps to the sixteen cubits of the Nile's rising. Her limbs are covered with a close fitting cloth, like that of a mummy, divided into various compartments, all of which, with the arms and shoulders, are ornamented with half figures of various animals, as, winged sphynxes, lions, bulls, stags, bees, flowers. This statue is a mystic representation of the παντιολως φυσις the ever varying nature, the nurse of all living things. The mere addition of a wreath, and the wall crown on the head, could change her into Cybele,

the mother of universal fecundity. The ornaments of the nimbus or disk, allude to the Sun or Moon. Four figures probably the four Seasons, with the signs of the Zodiac and a collar of acorns, adorn her neck. This remarkable statue was found at *Adrian's Villa.*

82. Sepulchral urn representing the DEATH OF CLYTEMNESTRA AND ÆGISTHUS. Orestes may be seen in the centre killing his mother, and Ægisthus is being cast from the throne by Pylades. On another part of the urn, we see Furies with torches and serpents persecuting the matricide, who again is represented clasping the Delphic tripod, and a branch of laurel, after the expiation of his crime. A nymph holds a lighted torch to the ground, in order to extinguish it as a testimony of his pardon.

83-84. Bacchus — Cinerary Urn standing on an altar with inscription referring to its dedication to the *College of Concord by Q. Ordio Pannicus.*

85. Small statue of ROME PERSONIFIED, sitting with a short Amazon's dress the breast uncovered, holding a globe in one hand and a she-wolf on her helmet.

86-89. Vase in white marble — Bathing Nymph.

87. Phrygian slave, carrying a vase on his shoulders.

88. Mercury seated, with many of his emblems and attributes. A small statue.

90. CUP in white marble, supported by three kneeling Sileni, bearing wine-skins on their sheulders. A very fanciful composition. It served as a decoration of a fountain, the water flowing out

from the bags. It was discovered in the excavations of *Roma Vecchia on the Appian* Way.

91. See N.″ 86.

92-94. Philosopher — Colossal foot.

93-97. *On each side*: TWO ELEGANT CAN-
DELABRA, adorned with beautiful arabesques,
festoons of flowers, and leaves of acanthus.
Brought from the Church of Sta. Costantia.

98-99. Child with torches in each hand — Foot
in *fiorito* alabaster, and white marble.

100. ELEGANT CINERARY URN, ornamented
with fine engravings of fishes, sea-corals, masks,
and festoons.

101-102. Fragment of a statue — Child caressing a goose, a small statue standing on the cinerary urn of *Pompeius Euperianus.*

103-104. Adrian — Child with the Eagle, undoubtedly Ganymede.

105-106. Fragment — Cup of white marble.

107-108. Vase in *pietra di monte* — Genius of
Hercules.

109-110. Cinerary Vase standing on an altar
with inscription of *C. Marsentus Plebeius.*

111. Mercury holding a dog.

112. Sarcophagus, exhibiting on its front the
history of PROTESILAUS 'AND LAODAMIA. It
is divided into various scenes the first of which
represents the corpse of Protesilaus lying on the
Trojan soil where he first landed, and where he
was the first one killed by Hector. Secondly,
Protesilaus is conducted by Mercury and restored
to the love of his faithful wife Laodamia, who is
holding in her hands her busband's portrait.

Lastly his shoul is also seen brought back to
Pluto by Mercury, paying in advance the *obolus*,
the coin for the passage of the Lethe, to the
miser ferryman Charon. On one side of the sarcophagus are represented the myths of Ixion, fastened in Hell to a wheel perpetually rolling, Sisiphus rolling the stone up the mountain, and
lastly the punishment of the ever-thirsting Tan-
talus. It came from the *Barberini Gallery*.

Over the sarcophagus are: Two vases of
white and black oriental granite, and of *verde of
Ponsevera*.

113-114. Cupid — Cinerary Vase on a base
sculptured by *Franzoni*.

115-116. The Infant Bacchus — Cinerary Vase
with beautiful carvings.

117-118. Children pouring water. They served
as ornaments to some fountain. Found on the Celian, and Adrian's villa.

119. Ganymede with the Eagle.

120. GRACEFUL TRIPOD in a very rare and
beautiful oriental rose alabaster, with diaphanous
veins and spots.

121. Cinerary Vase bearing an inscription to
Aurelio Victorio.

122. Sciateric clock, with Greek inscriptions of
the signs of the zodiac, and of the months.

123. Vase of a *porfido nero serpentino*.

Third Division.

In this division are collected all antique objects
discovered at *Tor Marancio* near the Appian

Way, about two miles from the *Porta S. Sebastiano*, during the excavations made there by the
Duchess of Chablais, afterwards presented to
Pius VI. They consist of frescoes in the Pompeian
style, a mosaic piece, busts, and statues. The three
most remarkable statues, are those of *Somnus*
which has been removed here from the *Chiaramonti Museum*, the group of *Bacchus* and a Faun
lately found, and that of another *Bacchus*, all
placed in front of the window.

The life-size statue of SOMNUS, or according
to *Visconti* of the GENIUS OF DEATH is represented under the poetical reposing figure of a
Cupid, with the head drooping over his left shoulder. The right arm leans aginst the trunk of a
tree, while in the left he holds a lighted torch,
the flame of which is turned towards an altar.

In the middle : FAUN AND BACCHUS. A
life-size group, found in the neighbourhood of ·
S. Giovanni in Laterano, skilfully restored in the
greater part by *Sig. Galli.* It represents the infant
Bacchus brought astride on the shoulders of a
Faun, in the act of gracefully removing the cup,
which the tired Faun presents to him.

124-125. Hermes bifrons of Bacchus and Libera-
Unknown statue.

126-127. Votive monument with a serpent, a
symbol of immortality — Head of Ariadne.

128-129-130. Torse — Nymph — Fragment of a
Praefica.

131. A variously coloured MOSAIC PIECE,
which decorated the floor of an ancient dining-
room. On it are tastefully represented vegetables,

and maritime productions, as a bunch of asparagus, dates, fruits, fishes, and a fowl.

132-133. Torse of Venus Anadiomene — Silenus riding on a goat.

134. SOPHOCLES. A small statue. It bears a great likeness to that admirable one which stands in the Lateran Museum.

135-236. Fragment — Faun smiling.

137-138: An oil merchant's shop — A basrelief.

139-140. Male bust — Socrates. Herma-bust.

141. *In the niche :* Colossal statue of Bacchus, with many of his attributes.

142-143. Marble table with a foot-print, allusive to the possession of a sepulchre — Flamen.

144-145. Fragments.

146-147-148. Sarcophagus with the games of the Circus — Fragments.

149. Bacchus. A statue smaller than life.

Opposite this statue : COLUMN in *fiorito* alabaster of the finest kind, found in the *Roman Forum.* On its top is a CUP in oriental *cotognino* alabaster, discovered on the *Appian Way.*

150-151-152. Fragmentary statues.

153-154-155. Bacchus — Sepulchral Covering.— Double Hermes of Bacchus and Libera.

Set round the wall of this compartment there are :

Eight small ancient FRESCOES representing Satyrs and Bacchantes, half clothed in loose flowing mantles. Some are playing on cymbals, others hold the wands of Bacchus namely cornucopiae, thirsi, flower-baskets, and torches.

Fourth Division.

Left and right side : Two fine VASES of *verde of Ponsevera.*

158. Genius of Death with a torch, and a wreath of flowers.

159. Vase in *verde di Genora*, resting on a block of *ghiacciuolo* alabaster and an Altar with ornaments.

160. Bacchus and Ariadne, found near *Montero-tondo.*

A. 160-161. Naval Victory — Small statue standing on a trophy adorned with Shells, and Dolphins.

163. Silenus, a small statue.

164. Cinerary vase of *Circereius Cotilus* with a Greek inscription to *Commodus.*

165. See N.ᵒʳ 163.

166. Candelabra with ornaments of leaves. Probably from some symbols of Diana sculptured in basrelief on the base, it was dedicated to that Goddess.

167. Nymph holding a shell.

168. Roman Lady closely enveloped in a drapery like Polyhymnia. Found on the *Cassian Way.*

169. Child with a bird.

170. Mercury, a little statue, represented with all its attributes.

171. Vase of Oriental alabaster.

172. Little statue, supposed to represent the God of Convalescence.

173. The founding of Ariadne by Bacchus.

174. Child with a military trophy,

175. LARGE VASE with a cover in white marble ornamented with carvings of grapes, vine leaves, and various dancing Bacchic figures in good style. On the *puteale*, or large mouth of a well on which the vase stands, are represented in basrelief, the daughters of Danaus drawing waters in pitchers, and Oknus weaving the rope of green rushes, while an ass devours it.

176-178. Dancing Fauns with the *crotala*.

177- *In the niche:* OLD MAN, holding a basket in his left hand. *Winckelmann* supposes him to be *Seneca*, but *Visconti* considers him to be a fisherman, from the fishes he holds in the vase. It was restored by *Algardi*. Discovered in the *Pamphili Villa*.

179. Large Vase in white marble.

180. Infant Mercury, found at *Tivoli*.

181-196. Two oval Cups of *rosso antico*.

182. Terpsichore with the harpe and *plectrum*.

183. Fragment of a statue of a veiled SATURN · in *pietra di monte*. Statues representative of this deity are very rare to be met with, the only known ones being the present and a bust in the *Hall of Busts*. It formerly stood close to the *Massimo Palace*.

184. ANTIOCH, personified, with the river god of Orontes at her feet. A valuable statue found in the *farm of Quadraro*, outside the Gate of *St. John Lateran*.

185. Very elegant Vase in the form of a bell, with double handles in *verde of Carrara*.

186. Statue of Somnus.

187. CANDELABRUM found in the *Verospi Villa* near the Gardens of Sallust. The basreliefs round the triangular aræ of the base exhibit a representation of Hercules carrying off the tripod of Delphi, also the figures of Apollo and a priest.

188. Vase in a rare alabaster of *Orte*.

189. *On the left hand:* Vase of a red jasper, made like a net. It is the only one of its kind, in the present collection.

190. CANDELABRA, discovered at Naples, beautifully adorned with *rosettes*, acanthus leaves, and various dancing bacchic figures.

191. Comic Actor with a mask. Found in the *Mattei Villa*.

192. Vase of *a nero antico africano*. It stands on a column of white and black granite.

193. Richly engraved Vase in white marble, standing on a *puteale*, representing the ferrying of the shades to the infernal regions. Found outside the Flaminian Gate.

194. Child amusing himself with a goose.

195. Infant shepherd holding some fruits, and the *pedum*.

196. See N.ᵉʳ 181.

197. Comic actor with the mask.

198-199. Vase in white marble — Satyr.

200. Jupiter under the appearance of Diana or *Apollo*.

201-202. Satyr — Vase in oriental alabaster.

204. LARGE SARCOPHAGUS exhibiting, on its front in basrelief the slaughter of the Niobides. At each side of the sarcophagus, Apollo and Diana stand in the act of shooting their ar-

180

rows on the unhappy Niobe and her sons. In the
centre of the group are old man and woman (perhaps Amphion and Niobe) trying in vain to save
their children from death, by pressing them against
their breast. On the frieze of the lid, we see the
extended corpses of the dead. The composition of
this monument, one of the finest remnants of antiquity in Rome, is admirable, and its execution
excellent. It was discovered in the *Villa Casali*
beyond the *Porta S. Sebastiano.*

205. Unknown statue, probably an Emperor.

206-207. Vase of Oriental *cotognino* alabaster
resting on an altar — Child.

208. *In the niche* : Life size statue of a ROMAN
YOUTH wearing the bulla. It is supposed to represent *Marcellus*, the nephew of *Augustus*. Found
in the excavations of *Otricoli.*

209. Child caressing a partridge.

210. Vase representing a Bacchic feast. On the
basement there are personnified the three cities
of Rome, Sicily, and Palermo, each represented
with her allegoric attributes.

211-212. Statue of a Child —Cinerary Urn fluted.

213. Child feeding a bird.

214. CHILD playing with a goose. We might
suppose this to be the group sculptured by *Boe-
tius of Charlage*, by its connection with the description given of the latter by *Pliny. Winckelmann* thinks it is a copy of that in the Capito-
line Museum. It was found at *Genzano* by the
lake of *Nemi.*

215. Fortune with a diadem.

216-218. Children in various attitudes.

217. Vase of *granito tigrato* of Egypt.

The urn on which it rests bears an inscription to *Pompeo Fausto*. Found in the villa of Cassius at *Tivoli*.

219. Candelabra discovered at St Agnes on the road to *Nomentum*.

220. Vase in *verde di Ponserera*.

Fifth Division.

221. Cup in *rosso antico*, with Genii holding garlands of flowers.

222. *Right side, in the niche:* A life-size statue of a young Lacedemonian girl, victorious at the Elian games. She is dressed in a short tunic tied across her person, leaving half the bosom and legs bare. The severity of style and execution of this statue, shows it to belong to a period earlier than that of Phidias.

223. Cup in white marble. Dancing Fauns and Menades are seen sculptured on its base.

224. Nemesis, the goddess of revenge.

225. Cinerary Urn in *palombino*, with inscription belonging to *Tiberio Claudio*.

226. Child with two birds.

227-228. Diana in the garb of chase.

229. Cinerary Urn of alabaster.

230. Vase of white marble representing chases of various animals. The *terminus* is dedicated to *Crescentilla* the wife of *Rogatus*, a matron of a proved honesty.

231. Sitting figure of a BUFFOON, wearing comic mask on his head Found at *Palestrina*.

232-233. Vase with interesting inscriptions — Poppea represented as Ceres.

234-237. Two CANDELABRA discovered at Otricoli. A pair of turtles is suspended by the legs to the spiral shaft of the one, probably sacred to the Dodonian Jupiter, Minerva, Apollo, and Venus. The other is adorned with grapes, leaves, arabesques, and birds catching insects.

235-236. *On each side:* Two Vases remarkable for beauty of form, and richness of their material, the *granatite stone*. They were brought to *Rome* from *Civitacastellana*, by order of *PIUS VI*.

238. Female statue holding a *patera*.

239. Crater of green porphyry with base of jasper, standing on a little altar dedicated to Æsculapius.

240. ETHIOPIAN attendant at the baths.

241. Vase in the form of a bell, discovered at *Ostia* by Mr *Fagan*.

242. Child in the act of declaming.

243-244. Ganymede with the eagle — Infant Bacchus.

245. Vase exhibiting in relief on its sides Marine Deities.

246. Youthful Faun, carrying a pitcher on one of the shoulders. Found at *Roma Vecchia*.

247. Cup in red granite, on an altar dedicated to Mithras.

248. LUCILLA wife of Lucius Verus, represented under the figure of Venus.

249. Cup of a rare black porphyry, resting on an altar with figures of some deities in relief.

183

Sixth Division.

250. *To the right side* : A finely wrought CRA-
TER in white marble, with reliefs of Neptune
surrounded by sea-horses.

251-252. Genius of Death — *Cantharus* in white
marble with a pillar of *porta santa*.

253. Sarcophagus with reliefs representing Diana on the mount Latmos, in the act of descending
from her chariot, to gaze upon the sleeping Endymion. Found in the *Casali villa*, outside *Porta
S. Sebastiano*.

254-255. Statue of Mars — Large Oval Vase
splendidy decorated with engravings.

256-257. Silenus found at *Roma Vecchia* — GA-
NIMEDE with the eagle, found at *Falerona*.

258-263. Little Child grasping a goose. Found
mear the *lake of Nemi*.

259. *In the niche:* DANCING FAUN, with
the *pardalys*, or tiger's skin, tied up to his
breast.

260-201. Faun — Paris.

262 Saturnus *bifrons* in *Pietra di Monte*, found
in the Massimo Palace.

263. Child with a goose.

264. Son of Niobe, a fragmentary but very
expressive statue.

265-266. Shepherd bearing a lamb.

267-268. Plenty — Vase of a fine Egyptian
bigio granitello.

269. A very interesting SARCOPHAGUS exhibiting the rape of the Daughters of Leucippus

king of Sicily, by Castor and Pollux. It was discovered in the *Villa Mattei*.

· *On the table*: Phrygian Soldier in the act of fighting.

On the cover of the sarcophagus, there are two cinevery urns, statues of warriors and a Fighting Gladiator.

270. Genius of Death.

Set in the wall above the Door Ner 6694. Tree draped male figures, holding scrolls — Vases with carvings.

271. Large Crater, with basrelief representing a rustic vintage by Fauns. Two of them are pressing grapes between two stones; another enlivens their labour with the sound of a double pipe. One hastens to carry to the rustic press, a heavy basket of grapes, while the drunken old Silenus is seen supported by one of his little companions.

GALLERY OF THE ARAZZI
OR TAPESTRIES

This interesting section of the Museum, contains the tapestries executed by *Raphaël* and his
pupils *Penni, Pierin del Vaga, Masaccio*, in the
time of Leo X, to adorn the walls of the Sixtine
Chapel, on festival days.

The Cartoons of these tapestries were
painted by Raphael in 1515, and afterwards sent
to *Arras in Flanders*, where they were copied on texture by Flemish artists under the
superintendence of *Van Orlay* and *Michael Co-*
cis, both pupils of Raphael. From tho town of
Arras, they have heen called *Arazzi*, under which
name, they are commonly known.

The history of these tapestries is a very singular. In the sack of Rome under *Bourbon* they
were carried off by the soldiers, but were restored by the *Constable of Montmorency* to Pope
Julius III in 1553 — During the French occupation
of the last century, some were carried off to Paris,
and afterwards they were returned to Pius VII, with other works of art. Some others were sold, and
fell into the hands of the Jews of *Genoa*, who
had already begun to burn them for the gold, with
which they are enriched, when *Card. Consalvi*
arived just in time to save them.

The Cartoons were bought by Charles I of England. After his death they were sold, but his son Charles repurchased them, and sent them to *Mortlake* to be copied, where William III, found them cut in stripes. to suit the convenience of the Artists. He had then entrusted them to be restored to *William Cook*, and finally placed in a Gallery at *Hampton Court.* They are seven in number viz: the miraculous draught of fishes , the charge to S. Peter; the death of Ananias, the healing of the lame man, St. Paul at Lystra, and St. Paul preaching in the Areopagus — Besides these there were others supposed to belong to the first series two of which are thought to be at present in *Turin.* Another forming a part of the Slaughter of the Innocents, was purchased by *M.ʳ Hael* an Englishman.

The entire series of these Tapestries according to *Vasari,* cost Leo X more than 70,000 *scudi.* During the fifteenth and sixteenth centuries they were exhibited to the public for three days, in the right portico of St Peters , at the festival of the *Corpus Christi.* After this , they were exposed for a few days in an apartment of the Pope. Lastly they were kept in the Pontifical wardrobe. After their having been sent back by the French Government, they were placed in this gallery by Pius VII, and Gregory XVI.

At present , owing to the munificence of the reigning Pontiff , they are in process of restoration under the superintendence of *Sig. Gentili* at the weaving establishment of St. Michael. The material of which they are composed is very rich, consisting of a mixture of whool and silk, interwoven with gold and silver.

Time and the accidents they met with, greatly injured them, and nearly destroyed the colours. Those that have been restored, appear as fresh and beautiful , as when they first came from the hands of *Van Orley.*

As to the order into which they are disposed, they are divided into two series, viz of the «*Scuola Vecchia* and *Scuola Nuova*» the Old and New Scool, referring to the early and later styles of painting of the great Master. Those of the first Series, are distinguished by their taste and skill of composition, which easily shows the hand of Raphael himself. The art displayed in the drawing of the second series does not exhibit the originality and skill peculiar to the first, as they were partly executed after the death of Raphael, by his Italian and Flemish pupils. To the latter are also attributed the landscapes and ornaments on the bords.

1st. Division.

Beginning on the left hand :

THE DEATH OE ANANIAS, who in punisheement of his falsehood, lies dead on the ground. Peter and John distribute to the faithful the alms from the common store.

The frieze represents the return of Card. Medici to his native country.

THE MIRACULOUS DRAUGHT OF FISHES. This is the first one designed by Raphael. Our Lord is seated in one of the boats. Peter kneels before him. Two of the fishermen, endevour with outstretched arms, to draw from the wather the nets full of fish.

SACRIFICE TO PAUL AND BARNABAS, taken in the change of Jupiter and Mercury in Lystra, after their healing the man born lame.

The socle represents Paul, taking leave of John, and the same teaching the Christians of Antioch.

PAUL PREACHING AT ATHENS, in the middle of the Areopagus. The different feelings with which the listeners receive the doctrines of the new Apostle, admirably express the various sects to which they belong.

The socle exhibits some events in the life of the Apostles.

The subjects of the two small ARAZZI wich next follow, are scenes from the Passion of our Lord, exhibited in three compartments, viz the procession to mount Calvary, the falling under the Cross, our Lord crucified between the two thieves, and the Annunciation of Gabriel to the Virgin.

Left hand:

THE CONVERSION OF PAUL, who is seen thrown from his horse to the ground, with the representation of our Lord appearing to him sur-. rounded by Angels. The composition is good. *The subject of the frieze is the massacre of the Spanish troops at Prato in 1512.*

THE HEALING OF THE LAME MAN by Peter and John, at the Beautiful Gate of the Temple, during the time of Prayer.

THE CHARGE TO PETER. Our Lord delivers to him the keys, instituting him the head of his Church, ad entrusting to him the care of his flock.

2nd Division.

Left side :

CHRIST appearing as a Gardener to the Magdelein, who astonished throws herself at the feet of her beloved Master.

CHRIST and the two disciples at Emmaus.

THE PRESENTATION IN THE TEMPLE. Mary and Joseph present to the High priest Simeon the Infant Jesus, with the poor offering of two tûrtles.

THE ADORATION OF THE SHEPHERDS. The Virgin kneels on one side of the cradle in which the infant Jesus lies, receiving the offerings of the Shepherds, who invited by the songs of the Angels, hasten to adore Him.

THE ASCENSION OF OUR LORD. The Apostles look astonished and desolate at the unexpected departure of their Master.

THE ADORATION OF THE KINGS. The lovely child sits on the knees of His mother, and receives the symbolic offerings ot the kings who guided hy the star, come to whorsip him.

Right side :

THE SLAUGHTER OF THE INNOCENTS ordered by Herod, represented in three touching episodes, each in a piece of tapestry.

THE RESURRECTION. Astonishement, confusion, and terror strike the soldiers who are placed to guard the sepulchre. The figure of Christ is exceedingly beautiful.

3rd Division.

THE DESCENT OF THE HOLY GHOST. The Apostles sit in the *Cenacolo*, and receive the Spirit promised by the Father. The Holy Virgin stands in the middle surrounded by two of her cousins, Mary Cleophes, and Mary Magdelein.

Right side:

THE STONING OF STEPHEN who has fallen to the ground, absorbed in the vision of Our Lord, who appears on the left side of his Father.

ALLEGORICAL REPRESENTATION of the PAPAL SOVEREIGNTY, designed by *Pierino del Vaga*. Two lions support a banner with the ensign and keys of the Church. Above in the bend of the rainbow are three figures viz: Religion, Charity, and Justice.

EARTHQUAKE, symbolically represented under the figure of a giant, who is seen in the act of shaking the earth, during the imprisonment of Paul at Philippi. The cartoon is lost.

GALLERY OF GEOGRAPHICAL MAPS

The colossal execution of these chorographi-
cal Maps of all the countries and provinces of
Italy was entrusted by Gregory XII, to the Do-
minican friar *Ignazio Dante* of *Perugia*, who
corresponded to the wish of the Pontif, by painting in *fresco* all parts of the *peninsula* on the
lateral walls of this Gallery. These skilfully arranged maps are placed according to their natural
order, viz on one side, Italy is bounded by the
Alps and the *Adriatic* sea, on the other by the
Mediterranean which extends as far as the country of the *Abruzzi* and of *Salento*.

The vault in the ceiling, is richly decorated
with fresco paintings, representing events from
the Old and New Testament, the lives of the
Saints and of the most illustrious men. The paintings were executed under *Circignani's Direction*
by several artists as *Lati, Mascherini, Semenza,
Massei, Paris, Nogari, Marco da Faenza, Giovanni da Modena, Raffaellino da Reggio*, and *An-
tonio Dante, the brother of Padre Ignazio*.

The walls round the windows and the maps,
are ornamented with festoons, fruits, arabesques,
and grotesques of great beauty. The fresco of the
vault in the middle of the Gallery, represents our
Saviour, entrusting the keys and the flock to
St Peter.

A rich collection of no less than seventy two hermes-busts of philosophers, orators, comedians, Fauns, etc. was by the munificence of Pius VII added to the Gallery.

Pope Urban VIII first caused the restoration of these paintings and maps, which had greatly suffered from damp. Afterwards having become nearly defaced by the loss of colours, they were restored to their former brightness by *Sig. Bianchini* and *Laïs* during the Pontificate of the present Pope Pius IX.

Beginning on the right side:

I. *Comp.* Map of the gulf of LEPANTUM, the ancient *Nepactum* on the Ionic sea, on the coast of the gulf. Near this place in 1571, the Christian fleet commanded by *Don Gior. d'Austria*, gained a victory over the Turkish fleet directed by *Perlan Pasha.*

II. *Comp.* TREMITAE, the island of Tremiti in the Adriatic sea, so called from the concussion of vulcanoes. It was formerly a celebrated Roman sea-port town.

III. *Comp.* SALENTUM, the province of Otranto with the maps of these towns.

IV. *Comp.* APULIA, on the Adriatic sea, an ancient Province of the kingdom of Naples.

V. *Comp.* APRUTIUM. A province of Naples on this side of the Apennines. The Samnium, a portion of its territory, is celebrated for the overthrow of the Romans at the Claudine prongs, as well as the lake of *Fucinus*, whose coasts were inhabited by the warlike tribes of the *Marsii.*

VI. *Comp.* ANCONITANUS AGER. The territory of *Ancona*, with a portion of the Picenum, the map of the town, and its harbour on the Adriatic sea.

VII. *Comp.* URBINI DUCATUS. The ancient duchy of *Urbino*, afterwards a delegation of the Roman States, with a portion of the *Picenum* and *Flaminia*.

IX. *Comp.* BONONIA with the town of *Rimini* and *Florence*. This country was so called from the paved road constructed by *F. Flaminius consul*, which extended from Rome to the town of *Rimini*, the ancient *Ariminum*.

X. *Comp.* FERRARLÆ DUCATUS, the ancient duchy of *Ferrara*, an eminent city of Italy, formerly a delegation of the papal Government, situated on the *Po*, and the Adriatic sea.

XI. *Comp.* MANTUA, the capital of the ancient duchy, a very important fortress and town on the *Mincio*. In its territory at the confluence of the river *Po* and the *Mincio* near *Governolo*, the Holy Pontiff Leo I. encountered *Attila*, and by the force of his eloquence, compelled him to relinquish his design of invading Rome.

XII. PLACENTIÆ ET PARMAÆ DUCATUS, formerly the dukedoms of *Parma* and *Piacenza*, with the exhibition of the maps of the cities. In this territory near the *Trebbia*, Hannibal gained the battle over the Romans commanded by *T. C. Scipio*, and *T. Sempronius C. C.*

XIII. FORUM JULII. The modern town of *Forlì* on the Adriatic sea.

194

XIV. TRANSPADANA VENETIARUM DITIO.
A province beyond the river *Po*, belonging to
Venice.

XV. PEDEMONTIUM ET MONSERRATUS.
The provinces of Piedmont, and Monserrato with
the Map of Turin, a part of the territory of Milan,
the Dauphiné, and the ancient duchy of Savoy.

XVI. ITALIA ANTIQUA.
All ancient Italy is
here graphically represented with its seas, viz the
Adriatic, the Ligusticum, or sea of Genoa, the
Ligusticum, or sea of Genoa, the Thyrrenum of
Tuscany, the Mediterranean, and a portion of the
Ionian. Its lakes of Trasimenum near *Perugia*, the
Fucinus, those of *Bolsena*, *Lugeus*, *Benacus*, *Ver-
banus*, the lake *Maggiore* in Lombardy, and the
Larius or lake of *Como*.

XVII. ANCONA. The Doric city, with its map,
and that of the port of Trajan.

XVIII. *Comp.* VENETIA. The picturesque city
of Venice the ancient queen of the sea, with
the several small islands on which it is constructed, and the perspective of a portion of its terri-
torry, and its chief momuments, as the church of
St. Mark, the Procuraties and the Ducal palace.

*The elegantly curved door at the end of this
Gallery, leads into the Halls where the Pope gives audiences, to the Halls of the Conception painted by Podesti, and those of the celebrated Frescoes by Raphael.*

Left side:

XIX. *Comp.* GENOA. Formerly the seat of the
illustrious Republic, now a province of the kin-

gdom of Italy. The prospect of the town built like an amphitheatre on the declivity of a hill, is
very fine.

XX. *Comp.* PORTUS TRAIANUS AD CEN-
TUMCELLAS. The town of *Civilarecchia* and its
sea port, on the coast of the Thyrennian sea, built by the emperor Trajan.

XXI. *Comp.* ITALIA NOVA. *New Italy.* This
map is the same as its opposite one, but arranged
in an inverted position, with the names of the
places in the Italian language.

XXII. *Comp.* LIGURIA, with Genoa its capital.

XXIII. *Comp.* ETRURIA. Tuscany celebrated
for wealth, culture of the fine arts, and commerce
It is situated on the Thyrennian sea, and exhibits
the maps of *Fiorenza, Siena,* and *Castel Miniato.*

XXIV. *Comp.* PERUSINUS AC TIPHERNAS,
Perugia, placed between *Umbria, Siena,* and *Florence.* Its lake, the *Thrasimenus,* is famous for
the defeat of the Romans by Hannibal, which happened near it.

XXV. *Comp.* PATRIMONIUM S. PETRI. The
patrimony of St. Peter, with the provinces of *Siena, Florence, Umbria, Sabina, Latium,* and the
Thyrrenian sea, the maps of *Viterbium, Urbsule-
tus, Rome.* the rivers *Pallia, Tiber, and Fiora.*

XXVI. UMBRIA. It anciently comprised a part
of the *Romagna,* the duchy of *Urbino,* part of
the patrimony of St Peter etc.

XXVII. *Comp.* LATIUM AND SABINA. *Latium*
anciently extended from the Tiber, to the pro-
montory of Circea at *Terracina.* It is now kno-

wn under the denomination of *Campagna Romana*.

XXIX. *Comp.* PRINCIPATUS SALERNI. The government of *Salerno*, a town in the same gulf, celebrated in the Middle Ages for its school of medicine.

XXX. LUCANIA, the ancient province of southern Italy between the *Mincio, the Thyrrenian Sea,* the gulf of *Taranto,* the *Apulia, Salerno,* and *Otranto*. At present it is known under the name of *Basilicata*.

XXXI. and XXXII *Comp.* CALABRIA CITERIOR AND ULTERIOR. Upper and Lower *Calabria*, between the Adriatic and the Thyrrenian seas.

XXXIII. *Comp.* CORSICA , the island in the Mediterranean, to the south of *Sardinia,* between Tuscany and Genoa.

XXXIV. *Comp.* SARDINIA, *Sardegna,* a large island, deriving its denomination from *Sardus* the chief of the Lybian colonists , who first inhabited it.

XXVVI. *Comp.* SICILIA, so called from king Siculus , or also *Trinacria* from its triangular form.

XXXVI. *Comp.* AVENIONENSIS DITIO. The town of *Avignone* on the Rhône in France. Although this town does not belong to Italy, yet it has been here represented, as it was for some time the seat of the Roman Pontifs.

XXXVII. *Comp.* ILVA - *Elba* - The island in the Mediterranean sea, with the Roman port constructed by *Claudius*. It is celebrated as the dwelling place of Napoleon, banished there in 1814.

XXXVIII. MELITA , *Malta*. Its delivery from the hands of the Turks who besieged it, is exhibited in the present and last compartment of these interesting Geographical Maps.

The works of art of this interesting Collection were brought here from various ancient towns of Etruria, as *Bomarzo*, *Todi*, *Volterra*, *Arezzo*, *Toscanella*, *Chiusi* etc. but more particulary from the necropoles of *Tarquinii*, *Vulci*, and *Caere*. We owe its formation to the love of Pope Gregory XVI, and lately of Pius IX, for Etruscan and Egyptian antiquities. The honorary inscription set in the wall, records the name of the first, as the Chief Founder of so rich a departement of art. The objects are placed in eleven Rooms or Halls in the following order. I shall point out the most remarkable:

Vestibule, or, First Room.

This room contains three terracotta sarcophagi, with figures of a young man and two etruscan ladies lying on their covers - Two horses heads in *nemphro or volcanic-tufa*, found at *Vulci* - Several interesting heads in terra cotta, brought from various places of Etruria.

2nd Room.

In this room are cinerary urns in alabaster *Volterra*, and sarcophagi in marble purchased from

Chiusi, *Castel Gandolfo*, and *Gualtieri' s house
in Orvieto*. - The more interesting one bears sculptured in high-relief on its cover, a recumbent figure of an Etruscan high-priest. The front of the
sarcophagus bears figures in basrelief of a very
archaic character. The other cinerary urns arranged round the walls, are adorned with basreliefs
representing funeral rites, Homeric deeds, and subjects from the Greek mythology. Their style of
workmanship demonstrates the decay of Etruscan
art. Above on the shelves there are numerous heads in terra cotta, some of which very interesting
for the remarkable expression of the portraits.

3rd Room.

In the centre: Large sarcophagus in nemphro
found at *Tarquinii*, the modern *Corneto*, in 1833.
On it reclines a beardless figure of a Lucumon,
both an Estruscan King and Priest. On the four
sides of the sarcophagus are sculptured various
subjects from greek mythology, as Eteocles and
Polynices slaying each other, Jocasta piercing herself with the sword, Antigones weeping, Clytemnestra stabbed by her son Orestes, Electra
mourning near the altar, Ægisthus lies dead on
the ground.

Near the window: Bust of a bridled horse in
volcanic stone; some urns found in *Toscanella*: A
travertine slab with a Latin, and Umbrian inscription, found at *Todi*. - A very interesting frieze
in *terra cotta* with heads of Bacchus and Ariadne,
between figures of Cupids holding festoons, fruits,

and arabesque works, discovered at *Cervetri*, and
.brought here in the month of November 1869 -
A bathing Nymph - At the corners of this room
are cinerary urns in the form of huts, still containing the ashes and the burnt bones of the
dead. They were discovered at *Castel Gandolfo*,
between *Marino* and *Genzano*.

4th Room.

In this room is a precious collection of terra-
cottas, which were partly excavated by *Sig. D'Agin-
court* and presented to the museum, partly were
taken from *Canova's* collection.

In the centre stands a finished statue of Mercury, very rare for its preservation. It is of Roman workmanship, and was found at *Tivoli*. A-
mong the other objects there are some *antefixae*,
vases, cinerary urns, ochreous legs; Faunus, or
Adonis lying on a rich bed, with a grey hound
on the base, it came from *Toscanella*; Several basreliefs relative to the labours of Hercules, a Victory stabbing a bull, and some heads discovered
for the most part in the excavations of *Cervetri*,
Vulci, *Veii*, and of the environs of *Rome*.

Fifth Room.

This room contains several vases of various
forms, of Etruscan, Greek, Egyptian, Babylonico-
Phoenician and Doric origin. The more interesting one stands in the middle of the room, on a half
pillar of Oriental alabaster, brought from *Vulci*

in 1835. It is a *crater*, « *vase for mixing wine* » of Greek form and style. On one side it represents Mercury consigning Bacchus to Silenus. On the reverse are three Nymphs celebrating the birth of the infant god. This vase belongs to the best style of ancient Greek ceremography. The 2nd vase, a *celebe* « *vase for mixing wine* » exhibits a combat between Greeks and Amazons. The other arranged on the shelves round the room are amphorae, « *vases for holding wine, oil, water* » They represent Greek and Etruscan mytological subjects as: Bacchic dances, the combat of Memnon and Achilles, Theseus binding the bull; Hercules and Minerva in a *quadriga*; Panathenaic subjects: Hercules fighting the Centaurs ; Europa on the back of Jupiter transformed into a bull, etc. The most remarkable ones are: an *amphora* placed in the middle shelf, called the *Poniatowski Vase*, representing Triptolemus in a chariot, wearing ears of corn, sent by Ceres to instruct mankind in agriculture. The other is an *oxybaphon* « *vase for mixing wine* » exhibiting a comical representation of the love of Jupiter and Alcmena · In the glass-case near the window are some glass-phialae, perfuming vases, cups, dishes, alabastrons , and balsamarii.

Sixth Room.

HALL OF THE APOLLO - *A square hall decorated with frescoes and mosaics. The vases in the centre are the most interesting.*
1st. Hydria « *vase for carrying water* » representing Apollo with Muses.

2nd. Ajax and Achilles *astragalizontes*, or,
playing at dices, the *astragali*. A greek inscription
gives us their names, as well as the numbers
thrown, *four, and three*. On the reverse is Pollux with a lance and his horse Kyllaros, Leda
with a branch of lotus flower, Tindarus caressing
the horse of Pollux, and Castor a dog; brought
from *Vulci* 1836.

' 3rd. The large vase of a globular form standing in the middle is an *holmos* or *therikleios*,
« *vase for perfumes.* » It is painted with squares
and scrolls, representing fabulous wild beasts,
and the chase of the Calydonian boar.

4th. Greek chief carrying from the camp on his
back, the dead body of Achilles, with Peleus
and Thetys.

5th. *Hydria.* Hector mortally wounded by Achilles; from *Vulci* 1836.

*The subjects of the Vases arranged on the
lateral shelves are the following. Beginning on
the right:*

3rd. *Amphora*, Hercules killing the Nemean
lion.

4th. Hercules contending with Apollo for the
tripod.

9th. Women running in the *palestra*, in a very
archaic style.

On the central shelf:

4th. *Hydria* from Vulci — Apollo seated on its
tripod in the Delphic sea.

5th. *Hydria*, with women carrying water at a
Doric fountain.

On the shelf between the two windows:

1st. *Kalpis* — The Calydonian boar hunt.

3rd. A boy with his tutor, supposed to be Ganymede and Jupiter. The tutor reproaches the boy for the stealing of the cock and hoop, which he holds in his hands.

4th. Combat between Ajax, Achilles and Æneas, painted on an *olpe,* a vase to contain ointments and perfumes.

In the cases of the windows are pottery articles, vases and alabastrons, in the form of quadrupeds, birds, ram's heads, as rhytons, kylices, « *vases for drinking,* » and bombylios, « *vases for ointment.* »

Hemicycle of the Garden della Pigna.

A semicircular gallery decorated with frescoes and busts of some pontiffs in b. r. Round the walls on shelves of marble, and half pillars in the niches there is a large collection of Vases of various sizes, excellently arranged. The most remarkable are the following :

Left side, 1st shelf: Amphora from *Caere* painted witw black figures on a yellow ground. Hercules is fighting against the triple Geryon. *2nd.* Hercules fighting against Cydnus, assisted by Mars, Hercules by Minerva. *3rd.* Aurora lamenting the death of her son Mnemmon, killed by Hector. His soul, already changed into a bird, is enjoying itself on the trees.

4th. Women filling vases at a fountain.

6th. Theseus killing the Minotaur.

2nd shelf. 1st. Achilles contending with Memnon for the body of Antilochus.

4th. Neptune seizing Aetra, who plucks flowers from a vase.

11th. Palestritae ; on the reverse of the vase, Minerva stands between two cocks.

The large amphora in the niche represents Hercules shaking hands with Minerva. *Vulci* 1837.

Opposite this, between two windows. Amphora, Hercules presenting himself at the gates of Hell, in company with Minerva.

Left side, 3rd shelf :

1st. A Pedotribe instructing a Discobolus.

3rd. Apollo Cytharaedus. *4th. Amphora from Caere* 1834. Hercules contending with Apollo for the tripod. Minerva comes un expectedly to terminate the struggle. *7th.* Cassandra striking a blow at Apollo with an axe.

9th. Neptune overthrowing Polybotes with a blow of his trident. *11th.* Hecuba presenting a goblet to Hector . Priamus stands by.

4th shelf. 1st. A Council of Gods. *4th. Stamnos,,* a vase for holding wine, or oil. Erecteus, with his wife, and daughters standing near an altar.

6th. Stamnos ; A noble assembly of Gods, as Jupiter, Juno, Minerva, Vulcan, Neptune, Venus, Pluto, and a winged Victory.

7th. Stamnos. Vulci 1838. Jupiter surprising Ægina. Her partners fly, and anxiously relate to Asopus his daughter's misfortune. Their names are written in Greek characters on the vase.

Opposite this shelf, between the two windows:

Pelice « a vase for wine, and oil.» Diana offering
a goblet to Apollo. Found at *Norcia.*

Gallery of the Tazze.

Besi les a great number of Etruscan and Greek
vases of various forms and colours, as *craters,*
œnochöes and *amphorae,* finely disposed in two
lateral ranges along the marble shelves, there is
also in this gallery a magnificent collection of
cups, *kylices, or cylices, «vases for drinking»* of
the most beautiful form, workmanship, and preservation. Expressions of joy, happiness, saluta-
tory expressions along with the names of the
artists, are inscribed on these graceful vases, with
the representations of various subject of Greek,
Pelasgic, and Etruscan mythology.

Beginning on the left, the more remarkable
subjects painted on the cups of the first shelf, are
the following:

1st. Armed warrior lying in wait; a bull led to
sacrifice, Men and women lying on festal couches,
Bacchantes and Fauns. *3rd. in the inside :* Ædipus
meditating on the enigma, proposed to him by
the Sphynx. *7th. In the inside :* Ædipus disguised
in a ridicolous form, and the Sphynx as a monkey.
9th. In the inside: Hercules crosses the waves
seated on the bow, he had received from Apollo.

The glazed shelf standing in the middle contains in its several compartments, curious Vases
exhibiting the figures of horses, bears, rams and
stags — heads, other made in the shape of Ethio-

pian, Egyptian, and Silenic faces—*2nd Comp.* Jupiter seated caressing Juno who stands before him — *3rd. Comp. Kylix*, Minerva obliges a monstruous dragon to rescue alive Jason. From *Caere 1834 — An Olpe, « vase for pouring wine »* from *Vulci* 1835. Menelaus taking vengeance on Helena who flies to the Palladium. A little Cupid and Venus meet with the Greek captain, whose sword falls from his hands.

On the 2nd. shelf. 11th. Neptune ravishing Proserpina.

In the niche at the end of the Gallery is the bust of Gregory XVI, tho founder of the present Museum.

On the opposite second shelf, left side:

5th vase, Midas with the ears of an ass, and the barber who discovers his secret.

3rd. Mercury standing in his cradle between two oxen, concealed by Maïa from Apollo's pursuit, from whom he had stolen the oxen confided to his care by Admetus.

3rd shelf, 5th vase: Triptolemus in the car of Ceres, drawn by winged horses — *4th. On the inside:* Prometheus is tied to a column whilst a vultur is tearing out his intestines. Beside him is Atlas supporting the sky, whilst a serpent rushes upon his side.

5th shelf, 1st vase: Cavaliers playing at dice, surrounded by their attendants. *4th. In the inside:* Achilles or Menelaus dragging the dead body of Patroclus.

Lining the left wall above, are arranged copies of the original paintings discovered in the
tombs of *Tarquinii.* They represent various Greek, Roman, and Pelasgic subjects as Cassandra
unarmed repulsing Ajax - Nestor and Phoenix -
Eteocles and Polynices, in the act of slaying each other - Achilles sacrificing Trojan warriors to
Patroclus - Servius Tullius releasing his country-
man Cælius Vibenna king of Etruria - A child
bearing a swallow in its hands - The Etruscan
Charon awaiting the souls - Sisiphus rolling the
stone on the stone on the shore of Acheros - lastly Amphiaraus, the keeper of the souls.

Hall of the bronzes

This Hall is decorated with fine frescoes, and
a beautifully ornamented ceiling. In this are collected objects in bronze, gold, and silver, nearly
all discovered at Cervetri in the sepulchre excavated by *Regolini,* and *Galassi,* in 1827. The first
object which attracts the attention of visitors on
entering the Hall, is the bronze statue of a warrior probably Mars, discovered at *Todi* in 1835.
At its sides are some tripods. Lining the walls
are suspended shields, arrows, helmets, spurs,
bronze mirrors, or *specula*, exhibiting mythological subjects as: Mercury and Minerva - Hercu-
cules Callinices, victor of Atlas - Aurora carrying
the dead body of her son Memnon.

Opposite is a funeral couch or bier with six legs of bronze, found at *Caere* in 1826; a child in bronze wearing a bulla , probably Thages.

Opposite the window is a bronze *cista mistica* , a casket of an oval form, found at *Vulci* in 1834. It is divided into five zones or bands representing a combat of the Amazons and Greeks. It contained bronze mirrors, bone-combs, and sundry other articles of a lady's toilette.   ·

A marvellous collection of silver and goldsmith's ware is contained in a large polygonal case, divided into various compartments. These objects were found for the most part in the *Regolini — Galassi* tomb , where they have been found buried with the body of the occupant of the tomb , an Etruscan princess styled *Mi Larthia.* Her name is recorded on the border of one of the silver vases. These valuable objects con-- sist of ear and seal-rings, *armillae,* or bracelets , cups, vases , dishes , neck-laces , breast-brooches, an oval amber-piece encircled by filigree, children's ornaments, bullae, *fibulae,* or, pins, several crowns of ivy, laurel, and oak, from *Praeneste* and *Ancona.* Which more particularly attracts the attention, is the gold breastplate divided in twelve bands, adorned with winged genii, human figures, and wild beasts *in riliero.*

In the glazed shelves and cases, at the four corners of the Hall, are vases, cammei, sacrificial instruments, domestic utensils, bronze-idols , statues of *Lararii* or household-gods, cauldron handles , lotus-flowers, plates, hatchets, knives , daggers; a small figure of *Minerva,* bearing an owl,

14

found at *Orte*, a little *cista:* some inkstands among which is a very interesting one in *terra cotta*, exhibiting an alphabet of 25 letters arranged in the most ancient form of Etruscan or Pelasgic characters.

Along the walls and on the marble shelves are bronzes, candlesticks, circular shields, among which the more remarkable is that one found at *Bomarzo*. It was purchased from *Sig.ʳ Ruggieri*, for a sum of 700 *scudi*. Some lance thrusts may be seen in it. It is supposed to belong to no later a period than twenty centuries ago. A similar one is kept by *Prince Borghese*. It was discovered suspended near the sarcophagus of its owner. Besides this, there are swords, poitrels, battle-axes etc. a *piticus*, or long curved trumpet. Below is a metal incense burner, or bronze-tray standing on four wheels, a bronze seat, and some lead pipes. Opposite, there is a brazier found in the tombs of Vulci, containing fire-tongs, rakes, and showels.

At the extremity of the hall are, a head supposed to represent *Trebonianus Gallus* - fragments of a statue, - a bronze colossal leg - the bronze colossal arm found at *Civilavecchia* in the dock. Colossal fragment of a dolphin, and a long spear-a war chariot in a very ancient Etruscan styles it was found at *Roma Vecchia*.

Next to the window is another bronze *cista mistica* ornamented with athletic basreliefs. Opposite the central window of the Hall there is a sexagonal glassed case in which are kept several objects sent from *Pompeii* to Pope Pius IX, by the king of Naples. They consist of coal, burned

straw, ashes, glass-vases, two stones for grinding
corn, and a basrelief in marble, representing Alexander the Great, riding Bucephalus.

*The small vestibule at the opposite extremity
of the Hall, filled with bronzes, vases, lead-pipes,
sarcophagi etc. leads to the:*

Hall of Paintings

The paintings arrange round the walls are
but copies of those, which adorn the sepulchral
cells or grottoes of Tarquinii, Vulci etc. executed
by *Sig. Camillo Ruspi.* They illustrate the Etruscan costumes, domestic and public manners, and
religious beliefs, as : banquets, games, dances, which have a funeral reference and symbolise the
bliss of the deceased. On some are palaestric games, as the races of the *biyae*, the chariots, with
red and black horses, having bleu and black tails
manes, and hoofs; also games on foot, as wrestling , racing , and boxing , girls dancing to the
sound of castanets ; Scenes devoted to banquets ;
representations of sacrifices with men and women
lying on rich couches, and leaning on double pil-
tows. Some symbolise the souls of the dead, enjoying pleasure in the Elysian groves here indicated by trees of olive, myrtle, lotus, and ivy. The
chaplets ,suspended to these trees, or hung from
the walls, show the custom of the ancients to crown themselves at banquets. Horses, hippocampi ,
tigers, panthers, snakes, and other animals, often
occur depicted on the entrance of the Etruscan tombs as to guard them , they are also emblematic

of the passage of the souls to another state of existence.

The order in which these paintings are disposed is as follows.

Beginning to the right side:

A woman performing the last offices to a dying man.

2nd. A funeral feast.

3rd. *Trapeza* or a cupboard. On a four legged table are vases, of different forms, with two *Camilli*, the attendants on the banquets.

4lh. The door of the grotto is ʾguarded above. by two panthers. Below there are two cavaliers on horseback, reposing from the race.

5th. Preparation for a funeral feast.

6th. Games on foot and on horseback.

7th. 8th. Citharista and Saltatrix, also a repetition of the funeral banquet.

9th. Youthful representation of a banquet scene, and dances.

10th. Two men on horseback, contending for the crowns hanging from the walls.

Beside the sundry Etruscan vases on the shelves of the Hall, there are also fluted brown jars, or pipes, which served to contain wine, oil, corn etc. A sepulchral *aedicula* of Ionic order from *Orte*, with the name of *Tanaquil*, inscribed on it. The pedestal of a statue bearing a latin inscription. It is very interesting as stating the date of 305. years B. C. It was dedicated by the Vulcentes to the *Nobilissimo Flavio, Valerio Severo.*

Returning into the Hall of Bronzes, at its right hand there is the last Chamber called of the

Tomb , for the fac-simile it exhibits of an Etru-scan Sepulchre.

Issuing from this in the middle of the cham-ber is a glazed case containing domestic utensils, found in the tomb of the *Heremnii* near *Bolsena*. On this case is a very singular case in bronze, of an Egyptian form, supposed to be a *Fumigator*, a perfuming pan.

The other objects are g'fts sent from *China* to His Holiness by Catholic Missionaries, consi-sting of two gilt wooden statues of Chinese in the act of praying, a bronze bell, and several other objects in gold and bronze.

EGYPTIAN MUSEUM

This Collection of Egyptian antiquities was formed by the munificence of Gregory XVI, from the monuments he received from Egypt, and from all others scattered in the Vatican Museum, in the Capitol and on various other places. It was ably arranged by *Ungarelli* and first opened to the public in 1836. The project of the Gallery was put in execution by *Cav. Fabris*, then director of the Muséum.

Vestibule or first Hall.

Two large sepulchral coffins in green basalt. On the cover of the one, some hieroglyphics of the linear class, record the names of the goddess Pascht, and that of her sacred scribe Psammeticus, secretary of the college of the Priests, and fourth king of the XXVI dynasty, about 554 years B. C. - At the corners of the Hall, in the glass cabinets there are two enormous mortuary cases with their covers, richly ornamented with paintings and hieroglyphics. In the one was preserved the mummy of Giotmut the mother of Chous Hierogrammateus, a priest of Ammon in the town of Thebes. The other contained the body of Manetes. They are both remarkable for the interesting scenes they exhibit of Egyptian sacred costumes, and mythology. The hieroglyphics with which they were adorned, are of the purest style, and bear the name of Amenoph I. with the date of 1832 years B. C.

From this we pass to the:

Hall of the monuments.

The most remarkable objects are two semicolossal statues of Pascht or Bubastes, the Egyptian Minerva. These and the four others in the hemicycle of the *Giardino della Pigna* were executed by order of Amenoph III. *Memnon I*, king of the XVII dynasty. They were brought from *Carnak*.

In the left side, in the middle: Fragment of the figure of Sesostris *Rhamses III*, seated on his throne with the date of 1594 B. C. The inscription on the plinth records his name; Torse of the king Nectanebo; Torse of a minister of the royal house, in alabaster of Gournah.

At the etremity of the Hall: Two lions in black breached granite. According to *Ungarelli*, they are worthy of particular note, as works of art. Found near the Pantheon in 1448. The hieroglyphics on the base, are of the purest Egyptian style. They were sculptured under Nectanebo, three centuries and a half B. C. The colossal statue of breached black granite standing in the middle, represents Twea the mother of Sesostris, *Rhamses III*.

Right side: Concheres", bust of the daughter of Twea. In the middle, is the portrait bust of Ptolemy Philadelphus sculptured 234 years B. C. This king is well known for the translation of

the Scriptures, called the *Septuagint*, made under
his auspices. *In the centre:* Colossal statues of the
goddess Neith - A statue of Arsinoe, the wife of
Ptolemy Philadelphus, discovered In the gardens
of *Sallust.*

3rd. Hall of Imitations.

This Hall contains the monuments of the so
called style of imitation , viz executed by Roman
and Greek artists , after those of Egypt. This is
the only collection known in the world - At the
bottom of the Hall, is a statue of Antinous belonging to the first class of art. He holds in both
hands the scourge, to drive profane persons from
the temple - Statues of Isis crowned with the
lotus-flower, and holding the *tau* and horns - The
Nile deified, in *palombino* or *bigio* marble. Isis and
Apis, a hermes bust in *nero antico* - Two naop-
heri, or Egyptian priests. Isis in an ædicula suckling Horus, seated on her knees, Sphynxes , and
crocodiles; head of a cow with a disc between its
horns. These objects were brought from Adrian's
Villa where they adorned the *Canopus* , an imitation of the temple sacred to Serapis in Egypt -
On a bracket above the Nile, is the bust of Gregory XVI, the founder of this Museum, by *Fabri.*

4th Room.

In the adjoining room there are Egyptian
works of art, as : A small statue of Menephtak
the husband of Twea, and the father of Sesostris
the Great, 1579. B. C. He holds the *tau* in his

right hand — Canopi or vases in calcareous stones. These served to contain the intestines of the
dead, after they were embalmed; A statue of
Abundance ; A naopherus priest ; the large inscription in hieroglyphic, with which it is covered,
refers to the succession of five kings, viz : the
Egyptian Apries, Amasis, Psammeticus and the
two Persian Cambises and Darius. Altar dedicated to Toutmosis with the form of the loaves of
bread, and channels for wine, the offerings made
to that deity — A priest with a cynocephalus —
An Egyptian hawk — Two leontocephalo statues.

Hemicycle of Belvedere.

This semicircular Hall contains four semicolossal statues of the goddess Pascht, executed
under Amenoph III, the eigth king of the XVIII.
dynasty 1860 years B. C. Some contain mummies
of conspicuous personages, both male and female.
One bears the name of Amenopht, written in gilt
characters, both a king and a priest of the XVII.
dynasty 1862 years B. C. Besides these there are
sundry coffins of mummies in wood and stone.
They were brought from Carnak, where they
adorned the road leading to the δρομος or temple of the city.

The best process known, used by Egyptians
to embalm their bodies, is as follows. The bodies
were washed with salt and water, anointed with
aromatic herbs and butter. Then opened with knives
made of obsidian, or Ethiopic stone, the entrails
were removed. They filled the remainder with wine

of palm, broken perfumes, myrrh, cassia, and all manner of drugs and spices. The body afterwards was dried with natron, and after seventy days it was wrapped with bands of a linen, with gum instead of glue. Lastly stamped with a type of a human being, it was kept in the sepulchral rooms, or wells.

Paintings, hieroglyphics and sculptures in low relief, which adorn the coffins and its covers, allude to the various states of souls after death. Head of the God Meris bearing the crown of Egypt; Fragment of an Egyptian Calendar. The mummy of Sonthos; that of Imopht, a priest of Ammon Ra — Two mummies of children; a female mummy with her portrait sculptured on the cover. Fragments of a column in the form of a lotus-flower.

The cabinet at the end of this semicircular corridor, contains various objects as vases for perfumes, funerary vases; large prints in a very curious form; several necklaces formed of scarabaei, and small idols in coloured stones etc. Hung to the wall, is an Ethiopian couch found in a sepulchre.

1st Cabinet.

In the glazed cabinets arranged round the ' walls, there are nummies of ibises, cats etc. several bronze mummies, idols, scarabei, a vase for the *aqua lustralis*, water of purification; some necklaces in enamel, painted glass, and earthenware.

2nd and 3rd Cabinet.

Among the various objects, the most remarkable one is the scarabæus in jasper, with an inscription of eleven lines, which states it was engraved in honour of the king Amenoph III, the Memnon of the Greeks, to celebrate his marriage with Taïa. It records their names, and the happy state of Egypt at that period. It is the most ancient of all known, bearing the date of the fourth year of the kingdom of Memnon, being of no later period than 3558 years ago — Besides this, there are some inscriptions illustrated by *Rosellini* — A neck-lace brought from Gournah. On it is engraved the name of Renoubka, the most ancient king of the XVI dynasty, who lived about the time of Abraham — A bronze-sistrum, two mirrors, a cup with corn and oat, a vase for the holy water, the *aspergillum*, petrified wood, etc.

4th. Cabinet.

Thirty two papyri in the various Egyptian characters as the hieroglyphic, hieratic, and demotic, are arranged in the glass cases around . the walls. *Champollion Junior* has wisely divided Egyptian writing in these three, the sacred, that of the priests, and the popular. The hieroglyphics are divided into figurative, symbolic, and phonetic marks, or characters; the hieratics are but a simple abrevation of the hieroglyphics — The demotic is derived from hieratic, being nearly

all phonetic, few figurative, and symbolic. Some of
these papyri mention of various Egyptian kings,
as Rhamses XXI. the founder of the XIX dynasty, 1500 years B. C. — Psammeticus I fourth
king of the XXVI dynasty, 654 years B. C.
Ptolemy Philopator ; His name is written on a
papyrus in demotic character, with the date
of 219. years B. C. Some also relate to the funeral rites of Egypt, others to solemn judgments
held by Osyris, and the punishments inflicted on
wicked men.

5th Room.

Coptic, Sundry, Arabic, and Cuphic inscriptions are set in the walls above — A fragment of a stele, from Hermonthis — Tutmes IV of the XVII. dynasty making a libation
to a God, allusive to his purifications. — Some ste-
lae of Meris — The queen *Amenses* — A colossal
head in plaster — Statues of Trismegistos — The
king Osorchon making an offering to the God
Phrè — A stele in hasalt representing Nophrebai
worshipping Pthak — An inscription of Meris
from Mandù — A small stele recording the name
of Rhamses XIII centuries B. C. Fragment of
a pilaster with the name of Siphtak the husband
of Taosra 1496. years B. C. In the centre of the
room is the top of the obelisk erected in honour
of the king Tutmes, which is now in *Piazzu
Narona*, in the centre of the fountain — A small
and good specimen of an Egyptian pyramid — A
statue of Anubis — the Nile.

THE END.

www.ingramcontent.com/pod-product-compliance
Lightning Source LLC
Chambersburg PA
CBHW030323270326
41926CB00010B/1485